Get the Point!
A Fencer's Handbook

Charles Simonian
Ohio State University

KENDALL/HUNT PUBLISHING COMPANY
4050 Westmark Drive   Dubuque, Iowa 52002

Cover photo courtesy of Dr. Joseph S. Streb.

Contents

Preface

Drawing from my long involvement in fencing as a competitor, teacher, author, and coach at three universities, I want to share with you my experience and my ideas on learning to fence, competing, and teaching. This book was written for fencers of all skill levels ranging from complete beginners to experienced fencers. It should be especially useful as a text in physical education courses and other group learning situations, and it provides some guidance for novice coaches and instructors.

While the book serves as a manual for new fencers, its scope is much broader and offers chapters dealing with strategies which, along with numerous drills, should provide some food for thought for those readers who are already competent fencers. This sport is, after all, as much mental as it is physical, and it requires constant study in addition to practice.

Advanced fencers may wish to merely skim chapters 2–4 that deal with traditional, sometimes termed classical, fencing styles. They will find so-called modern competitive techniques covered in later chapters. I believe that beginners should be taught along classical lines for two reasons. One, many students have preconceived ideas of what fencing is like and might not respond well to a modern, athletic approach. Secondly, and unfortunately, most fencing students do not continue beyond a first course and would be best served by traditional instruction.

It is difficult to learn to fence just by reading this or any other book (can you name *any* sport that can be learned from a book?). For one thing, fencing movements are very fast and are hard to depict through still photographs, and word descriptions of the various skills require that you visualize unfamiliar actions. However, you and an equally motivated partner, with the complete equipment needed for safe fencing, can acquire the basics of the sport by carefully reading and practicing the skills in the order that they are presented. The time-tested progressions and drills I offer should benefit beginners learning on their own as well as physical education teachers who may not be experts at this sport but whose duties require that they teach a fencing class. Appendix F offers some guidance in class organization, lesson planning, and teaching methodology. Major skills or concepts are numbered to make class reading assignments easier.

If you are fortunate enough to have an instructor, do you need to read this book? Every book has something to offer, and I think that reading supplements and complements an instructor's training. I recommend that you read any and every fencing book that you can find, even outdated ones. Be aware, however, that some books are of value only to advanced, competitive fencers. They often assume that the reader is very dedicated to the sport and is willing to train, perhaps daily, somewhat following the European or East European models.

I make no claims to originality here, and you will not find any previously unknown offensive or defensive skills, nor any secret thrusts or universal parries. After all, fencing is an old sport that has been thoroughly dissected and brilliantly written about. What I do offer is a unique organization of foil skills presented pretty much in the order in which they can be most logically learned rather than in groups of unrelated skills as seem to be found in some other books of this type. Following each level of skill instruction is a chapter on the application of those skills to bouts.

I have purposely omitted a history of fencing because I felt it would be beyond the scope of the book. Fencing's past is rich and interesting and cannot be done justice by a summary treatment in two or three pages. Each aspect of fencing has its own separate history as, for example, the evolution of the various weapons from their roots in war through their involvement in dueling and on to the present Olympic styles. One could study the changes in body positions, footwork, forms of attacking, strategies, or rules, and how all of these have affected fashion and armor over the centuries. Some recommended sources that provide excellent coverage of fencing history are listed in the back of the book.

For the most part I have used English terms for the various skills and actions but have included many of the more important foreign terms either parenthetically or in the glossary. A problem faced by many authors is how to keep a book gender-neutral, and I have chosen to randomly use he/him/his or she/her/hers throughout the text.

This book emphasizes foil fencing, but chapters on saber and épée fencing are included to introduce the basic skills in those weapons and to round out the reader's understanding of the sport. Indeed some beginners might be better suited physically or temperamentally to saber or épée than to foil; however, it will not be a waste of time for them to first get a foundation in foil fencing. The basic footwork and many blade skills are similar in all three weapons as are many of the terms and strategies.

Here and there through the book you will find boxed sidebars containing notes that might be of interest to some readers but which are not essential for learning the sport. Some offer historic trivia while others describe basic physics principles or identify important anatomic aspects of fencing movements.

I received considerable help in preparing the book and would like to acknowledge some of those who made contributions. I am thankful to Dr. Joseph S. Streb, Dr. William Reuter, and Samuel Lillard, Esq. for their fine photography and to the fencers who posed for the photos: Betty Brown, Dr. Joseph S. Streb, Joseph T. Streb, Elizabeth Streb, Andrew Merritt, Thomas Geohagen, Joann Newton, Peter Rogers, and Diane Joyce. Helpful critiques of early drafts were given by Julia Keener, Karen Simonian, Betty Brown, Andrew Merritt, Doug Bliss, Dr. Joseph S. Streb, Dr. Steve Devor, and Dr. Jeffrey Wilson. My Ohio State secretary, Colleen Weaver, went out of her way to help me with printing and copying. Finally, I am indebted to my editor, Michelle Weaver, for her confidence and encouragement and to my project coordinator, Kimberly Terry, who shepherded my work through the editing and publication process.

Introduction

You must already have some interest in fencing or you would not be reading this book, so you don't need a sales pitch about why this is such an appealing sport. Those who are past the beginner level know that fencing is demanding, different, fun, great exercise, and mentally challenging. One feels the excitement of combat without the usual risks associated with fighting. The sport requires discipline yet allows for individuality and self-expression.

Fencing is intriguing, challenging, and pleasurable for both novices and the more advanced. It is appealing to women, men, youngsters, and seniors, and it can be practiced for a lifetime. Fencing allows for the expression of an individual's personality and for the development of a style suited to the fencer's build, age, temperament, and fitness level. Like many sports, it provides relief from everyday stresses and offers a chance to participate in safe and exhilarating combat. For youngsters, fencing can promote self-discipline and respect for others and can help develop physical condition, body control, and reflexes. In my own case, the sport has kept me fit, physically and mentally, and has given me the privilege of knowing many wonderful people.

My reasons for having started to fence many years ago are very likely different from yours. I cannot honestly say that I was influenced by the many swashbuckling movies that I saw as a youngster growing up in Manhattan. Although we did do our share of street fencing using wooden swords crudely fashioned from discarded orange crates, at that time it never occurred to me or my friends that fencing was a real sport and that a person could actually get instruction let alone one day become a teacher. The fact is that I probably would not have taken up fencing had not a new club been formed at the start of my college freshman year. An alumnus who was an accomplished foilsman had volunteered to instruct any interested students, and I gave it a try little knowing that it was going to change the course of my life. That coach, the late Madison Dods, was not only skilled (twelve time division champion) but was one of the finest gentlemen, both on and off the strip, that I have ever known and I owe a lot to him.

By the start of my sophomore year, the club was granted varsity team status, and I competed for three years and then some more after graduation in amateur meets in all three weapons. When Madie had to give up coaching to devote more time to his engineering business, the team was in danger of folding, so I took over as an unpaid part-time coach. That led to coaching the team full-time while also teaching physical education classes. My fencing and teaching abilities improved after I spent some time in New York City doing intensive study under several prominent masters.

Not long after, I applied for and received a graduate teaching assistantship at the University of Iowa where I coached the varsity team for two years while completing a master's degree in physical education. A dream coaching job opened up and was offered to me by The Ohio State University on the strength of a recommendation by the departing coach, Dr. Robert Kaplan (thank you, Bob!), and I did not hesitate to accept. I completed my doctoral studies there and stayed on as both a coach and a teacher of a variety of courses, such as sports biomechanics and kinesiology. I continue to receive tremendous satisfaction from teaching fencing to people of all ages at the club level and continue to learn, probably more from my students than they from me.

Regardless of why you have decided to take up fencing, when you cross blades with someone you will be totally absorbed in the bout, and the first touch that you cleanly land will be a thrill and a milestone. You will not be imagining yourself as Zorro or a musketeer, and you will not be thinking about what great exercise this is. Instead, you will be doing everything in your limited power to keep from getting hit and to figure out how to get past your partner's defense. There is so much to learn about the sport and its traditions, but if you stay with it, lasting enjoyment and fulfillment will follow. It is a lifetime sport without peer.

►►►Fencing is a participant rather than a spectator sport, and it was one of the original sports included in the first modern Olympics in 1896, which by the way were revived by a fencer, Baron de Coubertin. Much time and effort has been devoted by the international governing body to make the sport more television and spectator friendly but with limited success. The action is too fast and some rules are confusing for the general public to follow even with the electric scoring equipment used in all competitions. In addition, most sports writers have shown little interest in a sport that is so unfamiliar to them. However, that could change in the future because at the start of this century a number of young, talented American fencers have been winning international competitions on a regular basis and might eventually capture the attention of the sports media. At the Athens 2004 Olympics, Americans won gold and bronze medals in women's saber, marking the very first fencing U.S gold in one hundred years, and that feat did receive considerable media coverage.

If you have not already discovered it for yourself, you soon will find that modern fencing is quite unlike theatrical sword fighting which follows a script and has to be entertaining, and of course winners and losers are predetermined. Today's fencing styles are derived from days long past when real duels were fought, but lighter weapons, electronic scoring, and modern protective equipment allow for much faster action than would have been possible with the swords of old.

I expect that some readers have no competitive aspirations and want to learn to fence purely for recreation or exercise or for the graceful movements often associated with the sport. Indeed, fencing can be taught to achieve those worthwhile ends by the careful study of the skills in chapters 2 and 3.

I never refer to fencing as an art form; it is combat, pure and simple, between two armed protagonists. But the intent of course is to score touches and not to cause harm. Skill is more important than strength. This is a safe sport; foils are not sharp, and serious injury is rare. The objective is to touch your opponent without being hit yourself. Easy to say but pretty hard to do.

As in most sports, becoming a consistent winner requires some inherent talent which includes such attributes as quick reflexes, agility, and a certain fighting temperament. Being tall or left-handed are certainly advantages but are not guarantors of success. A good coach can bring out the best in you regardless of your stature or natural physical abilities. Also necessary to reach high levels are motivation, concentration, dedication and sacrifice (not to mention money for equipment, coaching, club membership fees, and travel costs to meets). It should be obvious that the frequency of practice is a key factor in how rapidly you will progress as a fencer. Not including the top tier of competitors, most fencers go to their clubs only once or twice a week. This often is due to the fact that many clubs are part-time and have floor space available for only a few hours a week.

It is usually best to learn fencing in a class situation because it is more economical of time and costs, and it is always more enjoyable to learn with others. A class provides a variety of partners with whom to practice and is generally more motivating. After completing a beginner course, students should consider taking private lessons which can be designed to meet individual needs.

Whether you will be fencing casually or seriously, you should first find a coach or master, which unfortunately might not be easy if you don't live in a good-sized city. All too often there is no opportunity to get into fencing because of the shortage of qualified instructors. Even in cities where there are clubs, it is difficult to locate them. The best source of club listings in your area can be had on the web site for the United States Fencing Association, www.usfencing.org. There you will also find links to a great deal of useful information ranging from rules to results to lists of equipment vendors. Visit as many clubs as you can to see which appears to be a good fit for you. Take a trial lesson or class from the instructor before committing to a membership.

There are no hard and fast rules about the best age at which to begin fencing, but my own experience has been that few youngsters under ten years have enough maturity to pick up the complex skills. One prominent author believes that no one should start before age thirteen or fourteen. I don't doubt that younger students have done very well, but I think that waiting a year or two to start won't do any harm and might prevent early "burnout." As to upper limits for beginning, I know that adults of any age can benefit from taking up the sport as long as the activity is moderated to the fitness level of the students. Ready to learn? Let's get started.

Getting Started:
Learning the Basics

In most class situations, it is traditionally the foil that is taught to beginners, in part because it gives a sound basis for later learning the other two weapons. Another reason might be that, compared with the other weapons, it is more economical for schools and clubs to teach foil fencing since less protective equipment is required.

In this chapter you will be learning the basic body skills such as the proper foil grip, the salute, the on-guard position, the advance, and the retreat, plus some important concepts and terms. Later you will be introduced to the rules, the strategies, and some of the mental aspects of fencing. Do not expect to fence after only a week or a month of instruction. How soon you can fence will depend on many factors, such as how long and how often you take lessons, and on how well you retain the material. Your goal is to develop a set of conditioned responses and some perfection of technique.

A Quick Overview

The **valid target** in foil is the torso, which is the body including the back (yes, a touch on the back does count) but not the arms, legs, or mask (fig. 1). In front, the target extends from the top of the jacket collar down to the groin lines, and in back, the target extends down to a horizontal line drawn between the tops of the hip bones. Touches can be scored only with the tip of the foil in a thrusting motion as though you were, theoretically at least, trying to puncture the opponent. Any touches made on non-valid target areas do not count; such touches cause the bout to stop.

A typical bout is for five touches with a time limit of three minutes. Fencers in all three weapons must stay within

Figure 1. *The Foil Target (covered by the fencer's gray lamé)*

the boundaries of the strip that is 14 meters long and 1.5 to 2 meters wide (46 feet by 6 feet). For electrically scored bouts, the strip has a metallic surface so that any touches made on it will be grounded and won't register on the scoring box. A referee officiates and awards points according to the rules as will be fully described in later chapters. You should know that, in competition, all bouts are fenced using electric scoring equipment, but beginners need be concerned only with the use of practice foils.

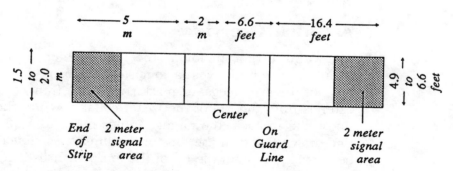

Foil strip measurements. Metric units (meters) are given on the left, English units (feet) on the right.

Figure 2. *Fencing Strip Dimensions*

1.   *Gripping the Foil*

Figure 3 shows the correct grip for the French and pistol grip foils. Notice that the thumb is on top of the handle and that the forefinger is directly beneath it about a half-inch from the thumb pad. The hand is in a natural "handshake" position and with the thumb at about one o'clock. The other three fingers lie flat against the French handle and not wrapped around as they would in holding a hammer. For class use, many instructors, me included, prefer that students use the French grip, but most competitive fencers use pistol grips for the added strength they provide in electric foil fencing.

The bend of the foil blade should be downward away from your thumb. A French handle for a right hander has a slight curve to the right providing a better fit against the palm. Some fencers prefer to hold the handle close to the pommel in order to get more reach, and while that is legal with a French handle, the small gain is offset by reduced control. Therefore, you should hold the foil as shown in the figure.

There is no need to grasp tightly because if you happen to be disarmed, the bout is stopped to permit you to regain control of the foil. More importantly, when using a French foil, you have to learn to manipulate the foil with your fingers, which you can't do if you are squeezing hard.

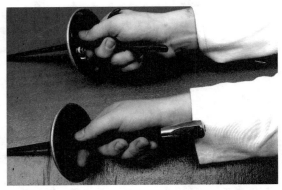

Figure 3.   *Holding a Belgian Pistol Grip Foil (top)
and Holding a French Foil*

2. *The Salute*

Saluting is a long-standing tradition in fencing and shows respect for your opponent and for the referee of the bout, and it should not be done in a slovenly manner. Start from an erect position facing your partner with your feet at right angles, your heels together, and your mask held in your non-fencing hand. Bring the foil to a vertical position with the bell guard at face level, as required by the rules. Then smartly extend your arm to a horizontal position and put on your mask. There are some elaborate, perhaps ostentatious, versions of the salute, which today are not common and should be avoided. At the other extreme are fencers whose salutes are barely recognizable as such. One seldom sees an erect, feet together, bell to face level salute these days, but beginners should certainly be taught to salute in the traditional manner. Note that saluting an opponent and the referee is required by the rules.

Figure 4. *The First Phase of the Salute*

3. On Guard Position

Get used to this position because you will be in it for most of every bout. A good on guard stance (in French it is *en garde*) will allow you to move forward or backward with ease and to launch your attacks, all without losing your balance. Figure 5 shows that the legs are bent and the knees are directly above their respective feet. The torso is erect with an equal amount of weight on each leg. The feet are at right angles with the heels in alignment and about 12 to 16 inches apart. Your head should face forward while your trunk is turned to show the least target to your adversary. However, don't exaggerate this rotation to the point of being uncomfortable.

The rear arm is shown here in the so-called *classic* position but you will find that many, if not most, competitive fencers have found their own way of holding that arm. I think that if you are a beginner you ought to at least start in the classic stance unless of course your instructor tells you otherwise. The rear arm, if placed correctly, keeps the shoulder back thereby exposing less target to the opponent. It also lessens the chance of illegally shielding the target with the rear hand and may help to maintain balance.

Figure 5. *The Classic On Guard Position*

Your foil arm should be bent at the elbow, which will be a few inches forward of your body. Your foil blade should be nearly horizontal and form a straight line with your forearm. Overall, your on guard stance should be comfortably suited to your build and will keep you ready to perform all the skills that follow. A more advanced fencer may occasionally have a tactical reason to shift his weight somewhat forward, but beginners are advised to maintain a well-centered position. Good posture is not just for appearance but is essential for balance.

4. *Footwork: Advance and Retreat*

All instruction from this point on is for right handers. Fencers constantly maneuver to maintain an ideal distance that affords the best position from which to attack or to defend. If you need to get a bit closer to your opponent, you will **advance** by taking a short step forward with your leading foot and then follow with a rear foot step of equal length. The advance may be broken down into two stages. First, the right heel touches the floor, and then the left foot completes its forward movement at the same instant that the right sole comes down. If done correctly, the spacing between your heels after an advance will be the same as before the advance, and your feet will be at right angles with the heels still aligned. It is always best to take short rather than long steps in the event that you need to suddenly reverse direction to avoid a possible attack by your opponent.

The **retreat** is even more important than the advance because you will often use it to back away from an attack; in fact it should be your primary means of defense. Start by stepping backward with your rear foot and then follow it immediately with a step of equal length by the front foot. Retreats ordinarily should be very short in length and very quick. If you need to make several in a row to get away from an aggressive opponent, your steps can be somewhat longer.

When you practice footwork, you should not neglect the proper maintenance of body and foot positions. All movements must be light and quiet, almost cat-like, since nothing is gained by stomping. There should be no rise and fall of the body during the advances or retreats.

Footwork Drill

A simple but effective drill for footwork involves pairing off with a fellow fencer to play the leader-follower game. Start by saluting and putting on your masks; jackets need not be worn since no touching will be done. The leader will advance or retreat in varying patterns and speeds. The follower will try to stay at a constant distance by moving in unison with the leader. At first the leader should move slowly. Then if the follower seems to be able to keep up with the leader, the footwork speed can be increased along with sudden changes of direction by the leader who now tries to "lose" the follower. It is very important that each partner helps the other by correcting any errors in position. These first lessons form the basis for all later skills, so don't let yourself or your partner develop any sloppy habits such as dragging the feet or moving from the hips instead of from the knees.

5. *Positions and Lines*

Positions are simply *locations* of the foil hand and do not involve offensive or defensive actions. Of the eight classic positions, the two most often used are the fourth and the sixth. When you are on guard, I recommend that you keep your foil hand in the **sixth** position which is to the right and in front of the bicep muscle. Your foil pommel should be close to the wrist so that there is a straight line from your elbow to the tip of the blade (see figure 5). In the **fourth** position, your foil hand will be in front of the left side of your chest with the wrist hyper-extended and the tip directed forward. You will find shortly that these positions will become parries when used to defend against attacks.

Lines refer to target areas on your body. There are four lines and they all relate to the position of your foil hand. A target area above the hand is referred to as the *high line* and the area below is the *low line*.

Your ***inside*** *high line* is your chest area to the left side of your foil, generally when your hand is in the sixth position. Any exposed target to the right of your foil is the ***outside*** *high line,* usually when you are in the fourth position. The *inside low line* is toward your left hip and the *outside low line* is toward the right hip. You can see that these lines can vary from moment to moment as you lift or lower your hand or move it from right to left.

6. *Engagements*

After saluting and putting on your mask, stand just far enough from your partner that your blades can make *contact*, that is, be **engaged**, at about their midpoints. The two important engagement numbers are **four** and **six** (not to be confused with *positions* four and six). As stated earlier, I will assume that both of you are right-handed in all of the drills and skill descriptions in this book. If your partner's blade is to the left of your own, then you are both in the **fourth** engagement. You will be in the **sixth** engagement if your partner's blade is to the right of yours. In the case of a right and left-handed pairing, then one will be in fourth engagement while the other is in sixth.

Engagement and Blade Control Drills

To learn to manipulate a foil with the fingers, one partner will remain stationary in a correct on guard stance, while the other will practice **changes of engagement** by passing her foil blade *under* that of the partner and then back up to make a light engagement on the opposite side. Try your best to move your foil

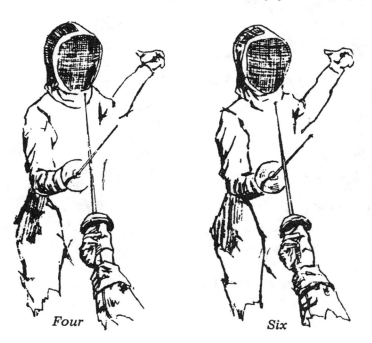

Four   *Six*

Figure 6. *The Fourth and the Sixth Engagements*

tip mostly with your fingers and perhaps a bit with your wrist. Do several changes in succession moving the blade in a path that is more vertical than it is circular. Note that in competition fencers seldom engage blades, and any contacts are generally incidental or are beats or parries as will be described later.

A variation of the drill for changing engagements involves carrying your partner's blade to the left or to the right thereby **closing a line** (a target area) to any potential direct attacks. To practice closing lines, the active partner will first change to a new engagement just before laterally moving her hand to carry the inactive partner's blade to either the fourth or sixth position. Then reverse and close the opposite line with the inactive partner offering only minimal resistance.

A similar drill has both partners each *alternately* closing a line by means of *circular* rather than lateral changes of engagement. When one partner has changed to a new closed engagement, the other will then in turn change and so on continuously. The blade movements are thus circular with one person engaging in sixth followed by the other engaging in fourth. After a series of these changes, reverse the directions of blade movements. To make it even more challenging, add footwork so that the engagement changes are being made during advances or retreats with one partner leading.

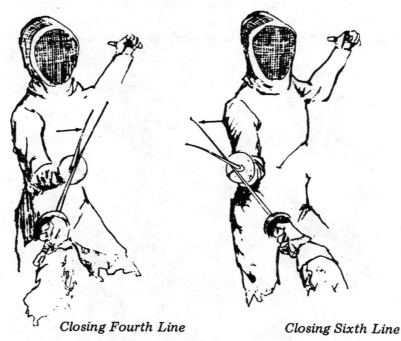

Closing Fourth Line   *Closing Sixth Line*

Figure 7. *Closing the Fourth and the Sixth Lines*

7. *Safety*

As you now are at a stage where you will be actively working with a partner in learning to hit and defend, it is necessary to be aware of safety considerations. Although foils are not sharp and the tips are covered, you must be constantly aware of the need to wear a mask and jacket whenever you practice. Accidents are rare if everyone in the fencing room uses common sense.

▶   Never point your foil at someone who is not wearing a mask.

▶   Blades do break occasionally, so be alert and stop fencing immediately if that happens.

▶   Do not fence with a blade that has kinks or weak spots.

▶   In class situations where students are often in close proximity, it is especially important that foils be pointed toward the floor during pauses in drills.

▶   When carrying your foil from one location to another, hold the foil by the middle of the blade with the tip up and the pommel near the floor.

▶   A sweatshirt is never a safe substitute for a fencing jacket.

▶   Anyone doing some competitive fencing must wear *full* uniforms, underarm protectors, and other related items such as chest guards for women as required by the rules.

Attacks and Defenses

Now, if you have gotten more comfortable with both the footwork and the handling of your foil, you are ready for more activity. It has to be emphasized that the material in chapter 2 and what you will learn in this chapter form the basis for your future success in fencing. You can never spend too much time in improving your footwork and lunge. Find a motivated, eager partner and read, practice, and reread the skill descriptions that follow.

8. The Thrust

As a lead-up to the next skill, you need to learn how to touch a partner and how it feels to be touched. With both partners **wearing masks and jackets,** engage blades in fourth, and decide who will be giving cues and who will do the **thrust.** The cue will simply be a lateral movement of the target partner's blade and hand a few inches to the right from a fourth *engagement* to a sixth *position,* thereby "opening the line or target." Upon seeing this signal, the other fencer, who should be close enough to do so, will extend his foil arm and will touch the partner on the chest. The touch should be smooth and not a jab, which could very well be an uncomfortable first experience at being touched, especially if the foil blade happens to be very stiff. When the touch is made, the blade will bend in an upward arc, the hand will be at shoulder height, and the elbow will be fully extended. You should not have to lean forward if you are standing at the correct distance.

In doing the first few hits, keep your tip on your partner's chest just long enough to assure that the blade has bent upward and that it was placed accurately. Not much force is needed for a hit to score. In a class, the double

Figure 8. *The Thrust*

circle formation is a good one for both this and the following skill (teachers see appendix F).

9. *The Lunge*

When you fence you will find that your opponent is normally too far away to simply reach out and hit. The most efficient way to deliver your touch is by means of the **lunge,** which is best learned without a partner. Start by moving your leading foot forward a few inches while also extending your foil arm. Return to on guard and then step out a little farther, being sure that your heel lands first. The rear foot should not move. After several repetitions, you will be stretched to your limits in a full lunge.

Now do the lunge in two distinct stages: first extend your foil arm with your hand at shoulder level; then lunge by straightening the rear knee while also swinging your rear arm in an arc to a horizontal position. At the end of a lunge the rear foot will be flat, the rear knee will be straight, and the left palm will face upward (see figure 9).

Pair off with your partner and stand at an appropriate distance from one another such that the target partner could not be hit with just an arm extension. As with any activity involving hitting a partner, masks and jackets must be worn. You will first engage in fourth and wait for your partner to give the same cue that was used for the thrust. When your partner exposes his target, extend your elbow with your hand at shoulder level, and aim your foil tip at his chest. The second phase is the delivery of the tip to the chest by fully extending the rear knee to move your body forward while simultaneously lifting the right foot, toes first, just enough to clear the floor. The lunge is completed when the right foot has landed, heel first, and is directly below the right knee. You should concurrently read Skill 10 on the **recovery.**

Figure 9. *The Lunge*

Good posture and balance are vital because if your lunge fails to hit, you have to be in position to return to on guard to avoid a possible counter attack by the defender. Unless you are flexible and have warmed up, make your initial lunges from a moderate distance to avoid tearing a muscle or injuring a ligament. Each time that you have completed a lunge, stay in that position long enough to check that:

▶   your front foot is pointed straight ahead,

▶   your rear foot has remained flat on the floor (rolling the foot is a common error),

▶   your rear knee is fully extended,

▶ your trunk is erect with perhaps a slight forward lean,

▶ your rear arm is more or less horizontal with your palm facing up,

▶ your balance is perfect,

▶ your lead knee is directly over the foot,

▶ your blade is bent in an upward arc as it touches the partner's chest, and

▶ your foil hand is at shoulder level.

Until you have achieved consistent and correct execution, continue to do the lunge as explained above in two distinct counts—extend, lunge. Also practice making lunges of varying lengths because every lunge does not have to be maximal. As you get better you can then combine the first and second counts, that is, start extending the foil arm while also lunging so that there is no pause between the two. Touch lightly and work on accuracy.

Consider your rear leg in the on-guard position to be a coil spring that is compressed and storing elastic potential energy due to the muscles being stretched. When you lunge, the rear knee extends, and the stored energy becomes kinetic energy to propel your body forward. It may now be clear why the legs must be kept well bent in the on guard position.

Drills for the Lunge

A drill that incorporates most of what you now know is the leader-follower footwork drill (Skill 4) with blades in the fourth engagement. The leader will occasionally stop moving, pause a second, and then give the target-exposing cue to lunge. As before, the follower should remain in the lunge position so that any flaws can be observed and corrected. The common mistakes in lunging could include:

▶ failure to begin extending the foil arm just before starting the lunge,

▶ failure to extend the rear knee or to swing the rear arm,

▶ failure to keep the rear foot flat (a short forward slide is permissible),

▶ failure to keep the right foot pointing straight forward,

▶ loss of balance caused by excessive leaning forward or to one side, and

▶ making a long lunge from close distance and possibly breaking the foil blade.

> ▶▶▶ **A bit of physics: Newton's 2nd law is expressed as a = F/m and states that when an unbalanced force (F) is applied to a mass (m), there will be an acceleration (a). Thus, in doing a lunge, your rear leg muscles exert force to accelerate your body toward the target. The 3rd law states that for every action there is an equal and opposite reaction. Your fencing shoe must provide adequate friction between the floor and the shoe to avoid slippage in lunging or recovering.**

It is not enough to be able to do a good lunge; you must also know *when* to do it. A simple drill for working on your lunge timing is to have your partner rhythmically step forward and backward, occasionally with a bent elbow, with the target exposed, and sometimes with an extended threatening foil arm. You should observe the pattern of movement and lunge only if your partner advances with a bent arm, but retreat if the blade presents a threat. Be patient; you need not lunge every time that your partner steps forward. When you attack, do so *during* the opponent's bent arm advance so that she would be less able to retreat from your lunge.

The lunge is so important that a fencer, new or advanced, must take whatever time is needed in perfecting it. Its length can be varied from short to very long, but not so long that you cannot recover quickly in the event that your attack fails to hit. The power and speed comes from the rapid extension of the rear leg and the length depends not only on the distance to be covered, but also on your flexibility. Some people are naturally supple and can make incredibly long lunges. Those who are not can work to increase lunge length through various stretching exercises, some of which are suggested in appendix E.

10. *Recovery from the Lunge*

Of course, you can't just practice lunges without having a way to get back on guard. That is where the **recovery** comes in; it should be learned right along with the lunge. From the lunge position, push with your right foot while you also bend the rear knee to move yourself back to on guard. As you perform these leg actions, both arms will return to their original places. The ability to make a quick recovery after a failed attack will help protect you from some counter action by your opponent. The recovery should be done crisply without dragging the lead foot, and it should be practiced as much as the lunge.

A less important variation is the **forward recovery,** in which the rear foot is brought forward to return you to on guard. This can be used if an attack has caused the defender to retreat a step or two and a normal recovery would only increase the distance between the fencers. After a forward recovery following a failed attack, a fencer might choose to make a second lunge if an opportunity to score presents itself.

11. *The Advance Lunge*

You have to accept the fact that when you begin to fence you will not score a hit every time you lunge. Your opponent just does not want to get hit and perhaps will choose to retreat a step or two when you attack. When faced with a retreating opponent, you can try an **advance lunge,** which is, as the name suggests, a combination of an advance followed immediately by a lunge. The advance portion should be very quick and short because taking a long step defeats the whole purpose of getting near the target rapidly. Your arm extension should start at the end of the advance; extending too soon will prematurely alert your opponent to defend. The advance lunge may also be used when your opponent prefers to fence at a distance which is beyond your lunging capability.

It is frequently necessary to make several advances before finally lunging at an opponent who relies on retreating to avoid being hit. If you are making multiple advances, begin extending your foil arm only at the end of the final advance before the lunge. You must know that a correct **attack** is, by definition, one that is made from lunge or advance lunge distance with the foil arm *extending* and the point traveling forward and threatening valid target. Read that important definition once again.

12. *The Parry*

You have learned that retreating is one way to prevent a touch, but an equally important defense is to use your foil to **parry** and deflect an attacker's blade. Of the eight simple parries, the two most important are **four** and **six.** As you learned in the section on engagements (skill 6), if the opponent's blade is to the left of your own at the time of contact, the engagement number is four. That numbering holds true for the parry as well.

To make an effective **parry four**, move your hand and foil *together* just a few inches to the left to the fourth position to divert the attacker's blade away from your inside high line. Done correctly, your elbow won't move, and your point will move horizontally a couple of inches further to the left than will your hand. To prevent your foil tip from traveling too far from your opponent's target area during your parry, hyperextend your wrist so that your pommel will end up separated from your wrist.

The **parry six** defends the outside high line and is done by moving your hand and blade to the right a few inches. The pommel will then be next to your now straightened wrist just where it would be in the sixth position. With either parry four or six, the point should be at about chin level and never too far from the opponent's target. Refer to figures 7a and 7b that depict closed line engagements but can also serve to illustrate the parries. The difference between closing a line and parrying is that the former is done to cover your target *before* an attack ever begins, while the latter is done when your open line is actually *being* attacked. In either case, the hand and blade end up in the same place.

Typical errors in parrying include:

▶ moving only the hand or only the foil point instead of both together;

▶ moving the blade downward instead of horizontally right or left;

▶ parrying much wider than is necessary to prevent a touch.

The thumb position in a parry should vary only slightly from its one o'clock position when on guard, perhaps ranging from a twelve o'clock thumb position in the parry four to two o'clock for the parry six. Note that figure 7 depicts only *instantaneous* positions when viewed as parries rather than as closed lines. Parries are seldom held in actual bouts.

Think of your body as being a goal, as in hockey or soccer, and your blade as being a goalie batting away all incoming attacks. Your hand must respond to any deceptions by quickly moving laterally from one parry to another and perhaps back again, and of course you can also combine parries with retreats or do whatever else it takes to avoid being touched (sorry, you are not allowed to turn and run).

Parry Drills

To practice both your lateral parries and your lunges, pair off with your partner and engage blades in fourth. Give a cue for the lunge by moving your hand to the sixth position to expose your inside high line, at which time your partner will lunge while you parry four to prevent the touch. Both of you should hold your positions briefly so that you can check on the correctness of your parry and of your partner's lunge.

This drill can later be done with footwork in which the leader will be the one who signals for the attack and makes the parry. But it must be stressed that when the leader stops moving, she should pause for a couple of seconds before giving the lunge cue so that the partner is not surprised in mid-movement and not ready to lunge. The same drill can be done using the sixth engagement and the sixth parry.

13. *The Riposte*

Having successfully defended yourself, now what? You get no points for parrying, so it is necessary to **riposte,** which is defined as the defender's attempt to score by thrusting immediately following a successful parry. A riposte can be made with or without a lunge depending on the distance to the target.

So, in summary, the opponent attacks you and you parry-riposte to get the point, unless your opponent has time to either parry your riposte or to recover from his lunge. Now you may be starting to see that the sport is getting complex and that you must do endless drills of the fundamentals in order to achieve some competency.

Riposte Drills

A simple exercise is for one partner to lunge on the usual cue and remain stationary while the other does a parry and a riposte, without lunging, to score on the cooperating attacker. A wide, sloppy parry moves the point too far from the target to permit a quick, accurate riposte, so whether parrying four or six, be sure that the point is always in position to hit the opponent's target. A common error in doing a riposte is to hit flat against the target, and this is often the result of a wide parry or a riposte made too quickly without aiming.

Two other drills can be useful to perfect the parries and ripostes. Pair off just beyond hit distance and alternately parry four and riposte without actually touching one another. The movements should be light and only as fast as you can both control, and there should not be any body motion. Both can then try adding lunges with their ripostes so that, alternately, one will lunge, the other will parry and lunge with a **counter-riposte** while the first will recover and parry. Keep the drill going continuously, but stop every few lunges to avoid fatigue and to discuss observed problems.

Most of your riposte drills should be done using the parry four because it is the most important and the riposte is easier for the beginner. In bouts you will of course need to use the parry six, but your opponent's foil arm is often in the way of a direct riposte and so some adjustment in the point of aim would be necessary, perhaps trying to hit the low line instead of the high line.

> ▶ ▶ ▶ **I often use the analogy of a tennis match. If the ball is served to you, you do not just stop it with your racket (your parry), but you stroke it back over the net (your riposte), and your partner does likewise until the rally ends with one or the other netting the ball, failing to return it, or hitting it outside the lines. However, unlike in tennis, you do not lose a point if you parry and fail to riposte.**

14. *The Priority Rule*

To really appreciate the skills we have covered so far, you need to know the basic rule of **priority,** which is known also as the **right of way.** The rule is intended to prevent the chaos that would result if the combatants could just freely poke away at one another. It simply states that the first person to start an attack (defined as the foil arm extending and the point threatening valid target) has the priority and this obligates the defender to either parry or retreat out of distance. If the attack is successfully parried, the defender now gains the right to riposte and the former attacker must then take defensive measures. It occasionally happens that two fencers lunge simultaneously with equal priority and each lands a touch; in such cases no point is awarded. But often the referee is able to identify the fencer who is at fault for causing a double hit and of course then gives the point to the opponent.

When a fencer is moving forward but is not in the act of executing a proper attack, he is said to be in **preparation.** The defender can "steal" the right of way by attacking before the opponent does, and his touch will count even if the opponent also simultaneously hits.

Note that priority is not an issue if only one fencer is actually hit, which means that even though the attacker started first correctly but missed, and the opponent incorrectly made a counter attack which hit, the defender's touch will count.

> ▶▶▶ The rule of priority could be compared with traffic laws governing intersections. A green light grants right of way to a driver. Should there be a collision, one or the other driver ran a red light or a stop sign and will be cited. The fencer who correctly attacks has "the green light" and if the opponent counter-attacks (causes the "collision"), he is at fault and the attacker is awarded the point.

A Brief Summary

Here are some things you should know by this time even though no one will expect that you can yet perform correctly and consistently:

- ▶ Your footwork should involve quick, short movements with no raising or lowering of the torso or dragging of the feet.

- ▶ You should be able to lunge without losing balance and to recover effortlessly and fully to an on guard position.

- ▶ When attacked, your initial response should be to retreat, especially when surprised by an opponent's attack, but when mentally prepared to defend, you should be able to effectively parry and riposte.

▶ You should be able to follow each parry with a direct, accurate riposte. A correct parry is, by definition, one that diverts, even for an instant, the incoming blade. It should not be held because the riposte, in most cases, must be immediate.

Now, perhaps you have already done some practice fencing and have become frustrated because the skills you have learned so far are not getting touches for you. You are, after all, still in elementary school with regard to your fencing education. Middle school follows, so read on.

15. *The Disengagement*

If your only form of attack is a direct lunge, you will discover that almost all of your efforts to land a touch will fail because it is too easy for a prepared defender to parry. So if you cannot hit in one line because a parry closes it, you will have to try to touch in the opposite line. To do this, you must resort to some subterfuge.

Start by making a threatening full extension of your foil arm into the open line in hopes of getting a parry response. To add the necessary realism, your **feint** of a direct attack should be accompanied by a lunge. Reacting to this perceived danger, your opponent will logically attempt to parry, and you must deceive that parry by moving your blade *under* the parry and into the newly opened line just before your lunge is completed. That deception, usually termed a **disengagement,** must be delivered by a fluid, powerful lunge so that you will touch before the defender realizes that she has been fooled.

Your deceiving action should be made with the fingers so as to move the tip in the smallest possible path under the defending blade while your arm is reaching full extension. The initial threatening extension is called a feint, that is, an action that looks like a real attack and compels the defender to parry. As you might imagine, if your feint is not believable (a faint feint, perhaps?), you won't get the desired response. If your deceptive effort is wide and therefore slow and obvious, the opponent will have time to reverse the direction of her parry and get back in time to stop your attack. As the attacker, you must avoid any blade contact which could be considered a parry.

It is likely that most of your feints will be made into the inside high line because many fencers stand on guard with the foil in the sixth position knowingly leaving the inside line open. The problem which that poses for you is that, after your deception under the defending foil, you have to direct your foil accurately over the defender's arm to touch her in the rather small outside high line. Because of that obstructing arm it is very hard to score with this attack. It is much easier to feint into the outside high line and deceive into the inside high line, but you have to deal with whatever situation you encounter. To add to your problems, your opponent may choose to retreat while also parrying your feint, in which case you will naturally have to deliver your disengaging attack with an advance lunge. This may be the most difficult offensive action in foil fencing, because its success depends first on your having correctly guessed what your opponent will do and then on your ability to time your disengagement to avoid the parry.

Disengagement Drills

In an obvious drill to achieve some skill at deceiving, you can work with a cooperative partner who will, from a *fourth position*, parry six at a slow speed while you feint to the outside high line, avoid the parry, and *then* lunge and touch on the newly exposed inside high target. As you improve your timing, try to make the feint and deception in one continuous, smooth manner followed by a strong lunge. The more difficult version of the same drill is done with the defender starting in the sixth position so that the touch will be on the outside high line after deceiving the attempted parry four.

Another drill has the defender standing in fourth position and ready to use a parry six if attacked directly. The offensive partner is assigned two choices: he can make a direct lunge or he can feint into the open high outside line and disengage. The defender will parry six only if she sees a direct attack and will otherwise hold the fourth position if she detects a disengagement. To keep the defender from just guessing, the attacker needs to make several direct lunges that will of course be parried. This is one of my favorite drills, because it helps the defender to learn to distinguish between direct and indirect attacks, and the attacker learns to make a convincing feint followed by an effective delivery of tip to target. The same drill is more difficult if the defender is in the sixth position.

16. *The One-Two*

A single deception attack may well be parried by a reasonably quick opponent who, having attempted to parry when you feinted, recognizes in time that the real attack is being made into the vacated open line and thus reverses direction to parry your final movement. So now you find yourself unable to score with either a direct lunge or with a simple deception. Don't give up, because for every parry pattern there is an appropriate way to penetrate. In this case you can try a **one-two,** meaning that you will make two disengagements.

Assuming your partner is in the sixth position, start with a feint into the open line to draw the initial lateral parry four, deceive that parry and then immediately make a second disengagement to avoid the parry six. The first feint must be convincing enough to get the whole thing started, and both deceiving movements by you must be made as close as possible to the defender's bell for maximum speed and effectiveness. The attacking blade must move ahead of the parry attempts so that no blade contact is made by the defender. Of course, your blade actions must be accompanied by an effective lunge.

The one-two is classified as a **compound attack** since it is made up of two movements as compared with a simple deception or a direct lunge. This term is of no immediate concern to the beginner but may be at a later stage. If you had to make three disengagements, which is rarely needed, then the name of the attack would be a one-two-three.

Some novices score lucky touches by using blade-waving versions of the one-two that confuse their opponents. Don't be satisfied with lucky points. You should use your foil to send a message ("look out, I'm going to hit you!") that causes an opponent to react, and then deliver the message with a lunge. A poor feint is an inarticulate statement that probably will not get the desired response.

Drills for the One-Two

The best drill for perfecting the one-two is similar to that used for the simple deception. Your partner will be in the sixth position and, when you make a feint of a straight attack, he will cooperate with a slow parry four, which you will deceive. Responding immediately to your disengagement, she will parry six, again slowly enough that you will be able to avoid that parry. At first do the one-two without lunging, and simply concentrate on making small, quick movements that stay ahead of the partner's parries.

Once you are both performing correctly, you can start lunging about the time that you make your second disengagement, and finally you should start the feint and do the one-two *during* the lunge. Beginners tend to make wide movements, unconvincing feints, or late lunges that allow an opponent time to make a third parry or to retreat. The feint should be directed fairly close to the partner's bell guard so that the tip won't have far to travel in deceiving the parries. Keep in mind that feints and disengaging movements must synchronize with and stay ahead of parry attempts. Should the defender "find" the attacking blade, he gains the priority and could riposte.

Because the one-two ends up with a touch on the inside high line, fencers find that it is a much easier attack to execute than is either a direct lunge or a lunge with a single deception. It should not be overused, however, because an experienced opponent will quickly make the adjustments needed to defend.

Earlier, I mentioned that the term **disengagement** is often used interchangeably, if not precisely, with **deception.** If your opponent has *engaged* your blade and has a line closed to your direct attack, you may then **disengage,** that is break contact, and direct your foil into the open opposite line while lunging; no prior feint is needed. A **deception** is a total avoidance of blade contact while a disengagement begins from contact. Don't let this confuse you because regardless of which word you use, the objective is to avoid one or more parries and to score a hit in an open line or a line that is *being* opened.

17. Circle Parry Six

You can now defend yourself with either of the simple lateral parries four or six or with combinations of these. However, if you limit yourself to just these skills, you may become predictable and your opponent will find ways to deceive your parries. So let's add some variety to your game—a **circle parry** can provide that variety.

This is sometimes called a **counter-parry,** but I think circle parry is more descriptive and also might avoid confusion with some other fencing terms such as counter-riposte, counter-time, and counter-attack. To do the circle parry six, start with your foil hand in the sixth position and your pommel next to your wrist. As your partner makes a direct lunge into your open high inside line, move your foil in a *clockwise* circle, passing it under your partner's blade and carrying it to a sixth parry. Make the circle by using your fingers, hand, and wrist rather than your whole arm. Your parry will start and finish in the sixth position by going through a full circle.

The circle parry is usually pre-meditated and surprises an attacker who may have been expecting the more common lateral parry four. If you use this parry sparingly, your opponent will have a real problem because you now have a number of defensive options. For example, when attacked you might stand still or step back, you might use a lateral parry or a circular parry, or do any combination of these. It's up to you to keep your opponent guessing. On the other hand, when you are the attacker, you should search for some predictability in your opponent's defensive tactics and take appropriate offensive action.

A circular parry is slower than a reflexive lateral parry, so it may be necessary to take a short step back to give you more time to complete it. Of course, your objective is not simply to stop an attack, but also to score a touch by riposting to whatever target is open to you.

Note that it is possible but not as common to do a **circle parry four** starting with your hand in the fourth position and rotating your blade in an *anti-clockwise* direction. That parry can be effective for at least three reasons. First, since it is a bit unusual, your opponent may not recognize it. Secondly, even if the attacker identifies your defense, a deceptive attempt always has some difficulty in getting over your foil arm to touch on your outside high line. Finally, it is easier to riposte from a fourth parry than from a sixth parry because the attacker presents a more open target.

The two most common errors in doing circle parries are making the movement with the whole arm instead of the hand and wrist and not being in the sixth position before parrying.

18. The Double

For every parry there has to be a way to get past it, and in dealing with a circle parry a fencer can use a **double,** a confusing term because it is not twice anything. (An alternate French pronunciation is *dooblay* when there is an accent mark over the *é* as in doublé). You begin with a feint of a direct attack into the open inside line, and as the opponent's anticipated circle parry six commences, you will lunge while moving your foil in an *anti-clockwise* direction just ahead of your opponent's parry attempt. Like the one-two, the double is considered to be a compound attack.

It is most important to make a convincing initial feint and to make the double with the smallest possible circle around your opponent's bell guard. Having made the feint, your arm should remain essentially extended until the completion of the attack. The difficulty with using doubles is in anticipating an opponent's circle parry. You cannot just reach out with a feint and then wait to see whether your opponent will use a simple parry or a circle parry. By the time you see the parry it will very likely be too late to deceive it. To touch an even moderately advanced fencer requires some keen observation of the opponent's parry patterns.

Drills for the Circle Parry and the Double

The following drill will be of benefit to both partners in learning to do the circular parry and the double. Your partner will start in the sixth position and you will extend your foil to threaten her open inside high line. As you do so, she will make a circle parry six while you lunge and allow the parry to succeed.

The next step is for you to begin as above, but this time you will deceive the parry with a double as you lunge and touch. Finally, you will have the choice of doing direct attacks or doubles, and your partner will be limited to doing either a circle parry or just remaining in the sixth position. When you really make a direct attack, then a circle parry six should be the response, but if you do not make a convincing feint, the partner will do nothing defensively and your poorly made double attempt will collide with the defending partner's stationary blade. The value of this drill is that the defender learns to differentiate between the real and the phony, while the attacker learns to convince the partner to make the circle parry. To keep your partner from just guessing as to your intentions, you should make several direct attacks in a row with only an occasional double.

> ▶ ▶ ▶ **I should explain that the traditional definition of a double assumes that the defender has a *closed line* engagement before the attack begins. The attacker would then start with a feint of a disengagement and follow it with a circular counter-disengagement to deceive the circular parry.**

Conclusion

At this point you have been introduced to the basic footwork, the direct lunge, two simple parries along with ripostes, the advance lunge, the deceiving of a simple parry, the one-two attack, the circle parry, and the double. You also know the fundamental rule of priority or right of way. Are you now ready to do a little more fencing? The answer of course depends on how well you have mastered the basic skills, how often you have been practicing, and most importantly, your instructor's opinion regarding your readiness.

It is best to delay bouting if you still lack adequate skills and self-confidence, but some early controlled fencing might serve to reinforce the need for patience, timing, accuracy, distance, and delivery. If trying too hard to win touches is resulting in sloppy performance, by all means stop and do more drills. Bad habits at this stage will be difficult to correct later, could cause blade breakage, or could even cause injury to you or to your practice partner.

The real fun in fencing comes only when your mind is free to develop the strategies needed to beat an opponent, but this requires that your skills are becoming so well-conditioned that you no longer have to think about your feet or your blade skills. The next chapter will present some bout strategies to study and put to use.

Self-Testing Questions

1. Against which anticipated defensive skill would you use a double?

2. What is the other name for "priority"?

3. Name two ways in which a fencer can get priority.

4. What is the difference between a closed line and a parry?

5. Describe the full foil target.

6. Since a circular parry is slower to complete than a lateral parry, why use it?

7. What are the numbers of the two most important lateral parries?

8. What is the purpose of a feint?

Your First Taste of Combat

Let's assume that you have learned the skills presented in the last two chapters and are now itching to cross swords with someone. Are you really ready? There is no formula to determine when the training wheels should come off. Skills alone are not sufficient; you must also develop a sense of tactics.

Having found a suitable partner, you salute, put on your mask, get on guard . . . then what? Well, for starters, you are facing someone who is not going to cooperate with you, as was the case when doing blade drills. There won't be any cues, and one of you will probably lunge and will fail to hit because the opponent (no longer a partner) will have either retreated or parried the attack. If your opponent is also a novice and just as uncertain as you as to what to do next, then I would suggest that you both agree beforehand to not be too competitive and to not keep score. At this stage winning a bout is not as important as keeping control, doing the skills correctly, and learning about your strengths and weaknesses.

The early bouts of beginners often deteriorate into somewhat primitive actions with wide parries and loss of form and balance. Observing these bouts may well exasperate an instructor who wonders what happened to all the skills that she has tried to teach. Think of these early efforts not so much as bouts but simply as advanced, unstructured drills. Limit your bouting to a fraction of your total time on the fencing floor, and devote most of your efforts to structured drills designed to correct technique flaws. With the proper mental attitude, drills don't have to be boring and can even be fun.

▶ ▶ ▶ In most sports the learning process involves not only the acquisition of skills but also the elimination of unneeded movements. Compare the smooth strokes of a competitive swimmer with the thrashing, splashing efforts of the beginner. Shed any non-productive actions that may be consuming your energy and interfering with your performance.

In many of the drills in chapter 3, it was suggested that partners should engage blades in order to be able to give cues and control the action, but in bouting you will seldom have the need or occasion to make any prolonged blade contact. To prevent your opponent from easily engaging or beating your foil, you should keep it moving in random patterns while remaining in the sixth position.

When you fence non-competitively with a partner, be sure that you both stop each time a touch lands anywhere and acknowledge touches made against you, whether on or off the target. Never call touches that you think you made on your opponent. It is up to the recipient of the hit to make that announcement, and if there is any doubt about whether the touch did or did not land, just fence it over.

▶ ▶ ▶ In the final fencing scene, Hamlet says "Another hit! What say you?" and Laertes acknowledges in his reply "A touch, a touch. I do confess't."

Without the benefit of electric foils, it is often difficult to tell if a hit was made with the point or landed flat. If both fencers are hit at nearly the same time, there is then the question of who had priority. You may be certain that you had right of way but, if your practice opponent is inclined to argue about it, be a good sport and give him the point; after all, there are no trophies at stake and in your own mind you know that the point was yours. At the end of a bout, remove your mask, salute your partner, and shake hands with the ungloved hand.

Fence with a wide variety of opponents and learn something from each. However, learning doesn't just happen; you must be able to identify how you scored your touches as well as how your opponents scored on you. Only by conscious study will you develop the all-important mental side of this sport.

Each and every fencer you face will present a different problem. One may be very strong and aggressive, while another may be more defensively minded. One may depend on quickness or athleticism, while another may rely on some physical attribute such as being tall or left-handed. Even if you are winning early bouts in your class because you happen to be athletic, fast, strong, and aggressive, you must still work on improving your technique and strategy. The real test of your fencing ability is whether you can defeat your opponent with your brains as well as with your blade.

> ▶▶▶ There are unwritten protocols that may vary from club to club regarding how to ask someone to fence with you. I suggest to my new club members that a less experienced, lower-rated fencer should politely ask a higher-rated member if he would care to fence a few touches. Do not be offended if he does not wish to. Perhaps the person is waiting to fence someone else or is tired at that moment. If you are the member being asked, try not to embarrass the person doing the asking. Give a brief reason why you can't fence just then, or state that perhaps later you will be happy to fence with her. However, if a more experienced fencer asks you to fence, never say no and be happy for the opportunity. Within a club there should not be any prima donnas who are above helping those who are still learning. Every top-level fencer was once a beginner and received a lot of assistance from others.

Some Thoughts about Offensive Tactics

▶   There is an old saying in sports that the best defense is a good offense. Usually, other things being equal, you are more likely to score touches offensively than with ripostes, so attack more often than your opponent does. I don't mean that you should throw caution to the winds and attack without using good judgment and timing. Play the odds and attack when you believe you have better than a fifty-fifty chance to score.

▶   When first facing a new opponent, you should feel out the opponent a bit by making a **false lunge,** which is simply a realistic but purposely short lunge. Your intent is to observe your opponent's reaction, if any, so that you can plan your real attack. For example, when you make a half-lunge, your opponent may respond with a very wide parry, and that would tell you that a simple feint and disengagement might work. I compare the false lunge to sending scouts out to get information about an enemy. Wars and games are often won or lost based on information or lack thereof. It is foolish to attack without a reasonable idea about how the opponent may defend.

▶   Remember that your opponent is also thinking and is aware that his response to your false lunge has given you reason to repeat the act and deceive his parry. It is probable that he will therefore react differently the next time by using a different parry or by retreating. So you might say that he now knows that you know, but does he know that you know that he knows that you know? Who will be the trapper and who will be trapped?

▶ It is much too difficult to hit someone who is on guard and fully prepared to retreat or parry, so you must look for opportunities, openings, and weaknesses. The best time to launch an attack is at the moment your opponent is advancing but not threatening. Direct attacks are often futile because, unless perfectly timed, they are so easily parried. The good news is that you yourself will not be easily hit with direct attacks providing that you do not lose your concentration or get too close to the opponent.

▶ But you will find that the compound attacks that work so well in practice drills are very hard to use in competition because they require analysis, perfect timing, and confident execution.

▶ Be very careful to not telegraph the start of your attacks. Some prior movements of your blade, leading foot, or body can serve to disguise when you will really act.

Some Thoughts about Defensive Tactics

▶ On defense, the key word is unpredictability. Do not use the same parry twice in a row. Your present skill repertoire includes the lateral parry four, the circle parry six, and the retreat. By using them all in varying patterns and combinations you will create real problems for an opponent.

▶ If you are easily hit with direct attacks, the fault may be in your being too close. Stay at a distance of your choosing; move in only when you are ready to attack.

▶ Use the retreat as your primary defense, especially if your opponent's attacks have been confusing you. By staying just out of distance, you may frustrate your opponent and cause her to lose patience and make an error in judgment that will give you an opportunity to attack or to parry and riposte on your terms. **Parry because you can, not because you must.**

▶ You don't get points for parrying; you have to riposte. A parry only takes away the attacker's priority and your riposte will have priority if you use it.

▶ It takes discipline to wait for the right moment to launch an attack. Patience is a virtue, but only up to a point because bouts have time limits and you may be forced to take action even when conditions are not favorable.

▶ A fundamental rule in sports is that if something is not working then change, but when your tactics are effective do not change.

It is natural to want to win (or to not lose), but self-control and technique improvement are your major goals. Fencing ultimately is based upon the principle of hitting and not being hit. You must choose the right skill to use and use it at the right time, and that ability can only be acquired with experience.

Even when you have a clear game plan, you have to be ready to strike when you detect an opening. There is usually only a small window of opportunity, and you must be set to take advantage of it. By that I mean you must be constantly focused mentally and well-positioned physically to attack or defend.

If you maintain correct distance and analyze your opponent's style, then you are less likely to be surprised by an attack that forces you into parrying reflexively. Be in charge of the bout and how it will be fought so that you can choose whether to retreat or to parry any particular attack.

How fast you will progress depends on many factors aside from a natural ability. Among these are the frequency and length of practice sessions, seriousness of purpose, and the quality of instruction you receive. College team fencers have many advantages over those who fence in clubs because they often can practice daily whereas the typical club fencer can practice only once or twice a week.

Lessons from a fencing master, or even from an experienced amateur, are necessary for improvement, but your willingness to work hard is also required. At this point your skills are limited. Just as a carpenter cannot build a house with only a hammer, pliers, and screwdriver, you too need more tools at your disposal. The skills in the next chapter will broaden your game both in terms of skills and strategies. Have fun and be a courteous opponent.

> ▶▶▶ **"The saying goes, Have a good hand, and you will touch sometimes. Have a good hand and good legs and you will touch often. Add a good head, and you will always touch."**
>
> **—An excerpt from French artist Paul Gauguin's *Intimate Journals*.**

The Intermediate
Level of Foil Skills

My classification of skills and strategies into categories such as beginning, intermediate, and advanced is clearly arbitrary, and teachers using this book are encouraged to mix and match as they wish. In typical courses, the content is largely determined by such factors as the number of class meetings and the length of time of each. The material covered through chapter 4 may well be all that can be included in a beginner course, but there are many more skills to be learned.

The additional skills in this chapter will enhance your offensive and defensive capabilities. By having a broader repertoire you will be better able to deal with the variety of styles that you will be facing on the strip. I want to emphasize, however, that knowing a lot of skills is not as important as being able to perform a few skills very well and at the right time.

19. Point in Line

The highest priority is that of a **point in line,** which is defined as having your foil arm fully extended in line with your foil and with your foil tip aimed at an opponent's target, generally a high line. If while you are in line your opponent is foolish enough to attack and become "impaled" on your foil tip, the point is yours even though the attack landed on you at about the same time. Imagine that two fencers had *sharp* foils. A direct attack against the one who was in line would result in two wounded fencers which is the fault of the attacker who, after all, did not have to lunge. (Then again, if you both had sharp foils, would you have kept your point in line and risked getting skewered just for the satisfaction of also having skewered the attacker? But this is a sport and not real combat, so there have to be rules.)

Any movements you might make such as advancing, retreating, or lunging, do not affect the priority of your line. Priority is lost if, while being attacked, you bend your foil arm, allow your point to stray out of line, or have your blade beaten by your opponent. You should use a point in line tactic sparingly, but it has value in dealing with certain difficult styles and can at least temporarily distract or force an aggressive opponent to shift his focus to dealing with your threat. When you face an opponent who has a point in line, you must find a way to divert that point, even for just an instant, in order to gain priority to attack.

20. Beat Attack

The most common means of taking priority from a point in line is to do a **beat** followed by a lunge. Just before you attack, relax the last three fingers to create a gap between your palm and the handle. Now by quickly closing your fingers, your foil should cause a sharp beat on the opponent's blade. Immediately extend your foil arm and lunge. Any delay after the beat might give your opponent time to parry or regain the line. When you beat, your blade must have enough angular contact with the opposing blade; otherwise you may make an extremely weak beat with the thin end (foible) of your blade against the strong (forte) part of your opponent's blade.

Naturally, a defender with a point in line knows that you will likely try to use a beat. She may plan to deceive your attempt to beat (a dérobement) and thereby remain in line and maintain priority. However, your beat will be very difficult to deceive so long as you do not telegraph your action by first winding up a bit. But the defender with a line also has the options of parrying your beat attack or retreating from your lunge.

While it is the fourth beat that is used most often, it is also the one that a defender in line is anticipating. You do have other choices, such as using 1) a sixth beat which is generally not very strong and is less commonly used because the wrist rather than the fingers are used and the target is somewhat obstructed by the opponent's foil arm; 2) a beat directed either upward or downward; or 3) a circular change beat in which your blade goes under that of the opponent and beats on the opposite side. Any of these can result in touches if done unexpectedly and explosively.

It should be noted that a beat attack could be used against a blade even when it is not in line, but from normal lunge distance such beat attacks are easily parried. The reason I did not include the beat in chapter 3 is that many beginners tend to overuse it when they fence elementary bouts. A beat is a fairly natural thing to do, but it alerts the opponent to parry or retreat since it is not only felt but is also seen and heard.

I like to use a beat with a false lunge at the start of a bout to get some information about my opponent's parry response or his hand strength. Against an opponent who is in line, I often use one or more beats without lunging as a means of harassment to send the message that I have no intention of attacking him. He most likely will tire of having his blade repeatedly beaten and will remove his point in line.

21. *Beat and Disengage*

Whenever you make a beat, you are in effect shocking your opponent into taking some action, typically a parry. If a parry response is what you expect, then your logical tactic is to use the beat as a feint to draw the parry, which you plan to deceive, and then score a touch in the newly opened line. Your choice of deceiving skill depends on the type of parry that you anticipate. For example, you might beat and do a double if you think that your opponent will respond to your beat with a circular parry, or a one-two can be used if you expect a lateral parry four-six combination. In any case, a powerful lunge must follow your deception.

If you sense that your opponent will not only parry but will retreat as well, you will of course use an advance with your beat and disengage while lunging. The timing of the beat depends upon how fast you are able to advance because you need time and room to successfully deceive the parry. If your advance is slow, then delay the beat to coincide with the movement of your rear foot in order to reduce the time between the beat and the disengagement.

22. *Beat Parry*

While a beat is normally an offensive tool, it can also be used defensively. A beat parry is generally premeditated based on your observation of the opponent's attacking style. It differs from the normal *opposition* or *blocking* parries described earlier in skill 12 in that it is done sooner and more crisply.

When you fence someone who comes toward you with a fully extended foil arm during an advance lunge, you can intercept the incoming blade by making a quick beat in fourth followed instantly by your extension to the target. The beat should start *during* the opponent's advance; if you wait until the lunge actually begins, you will probably have to use an opposition parry. The success of a beat parry depends upon your being able to maintain a long enough distance that your opponent is forced to use an advance lunge to reach you. Timed correctly, your beat parry will meet the incoming feint before the attacker can execute whatever blade skill he intended to use to hit you. You need not lunge since the opponent is coming toward you with some speed.

23. *Disengagement Riposte*

Unless you are quite quick with your ripostes, you might fail to hit because your opponent will naturally try to parry and make a counter-riposte. If your direct ripostes are being parried, you can resort to riposting indirectly by passing your blade under your opponent's parry attempt and scoring in the line opposite to the one in which you made the parry. This is not too difficult from a parry six but can be a problem following a parry four because the defender's arm presents an obstruction and there is a rather small target area available to hit. It is therefore often easier to hit by using a **one-two** riposte from a parry four since the touch will arrive on the more open inside high line after first threatening the outside line. In most situations, if a direct riposte is being parried, I advocate using the one-two rather than a single disengagement.

As with any riposte, you may or may not have to lunge. If your opponent remains in a lunge to defend with a parry, you should begin your disengaging riposte while your arm is still bent and then extend as you make the deceiving action. At such close distance, an attempt to disengage and riposte in a single action will usually fail to score because there is no room to deceive the parry and aim. Obviously, if your opponent usually recovers while parrying, you will lunge with your disengaging or one-two riposte in exactly the same way you would when attacking.

24. Cutover Attack (Coupé)

An alternative method of passing your blade to an opposite line during an attack is to move your foil *over* that of your opponent. While the disengaging action you learned earlier takes a shorter path to the target, the **cutover** often serves to surprise a defender because it is slower and less common. It can throw the defender's timing off and can be combined with disengagements if necessary.

A cutover begins with a raising of your point by use of fingers, wrist, and a little bending of the elbow. As soon as your point has passed over the tip of your opponent's foil, extend your foil arm into the opposite line while lunging. Be careful not to lift the point any higher than is necessary to clear the defending blade, and be very sure to fully extend on the down stroke; otherwise you might hit flat. In preparing to do a cutover, while still on guard, lift your tip a bit higher than usual so that it will not have to be raised as far when you start your attack.

The cutover is classified as a simple attack and is not difficult to parry, so you might have to resort to compound variations such as 1) feinting a cutover to one side and then doing a second cutover to the other side, or 2) disengaging after the first cutover. When making a cutover feint, be careful to make only a very shallow hint of a cutover so that you will have the time to complete the real cutover. Because of their complexity, compound attacks of any nature require more time to execute and so are generally most effective when making advance lunges rather than simple lunges. When you decide to make an advance lunge while using some type of compound action, do so very quickly to reduce the risk of being attacked into your preparation. Remember that priority is yours only when your blade is in its final threatening movement.

The cutover is often effective as a means of riposting indirectly. Instead of making a normal lateral parry four, try parrying by making the blade contact as the first part of a cutover, somewhat like a scraping, backward beat. Then, without pause, terminate the riposte to your opponent's low outside line. Unlike the vertical lift that starts an offensive cutover, the first phase here should actually be a diagonal rearward movement in the direction of your left shoulder as your parry is made. A cutover riposte can also be done after a circle parry six, which must be made without interruption and will usually touch very high on the opponent's inside line.

25. *Attacks to the Low Lines*

Although the majority of attacks are directed to the high lines, those lines are the ones that fencers generally have learned to defend pretty well. So if attacks to the larger high targets have not been working for you, try to touch the smaller target area lying below the defender's hand level. The nearest low target is the opponent's outside low line just above his right hip; you will less often aim at the low inside line. A simple lunge to the low line is made pretty much the same way that you would attack the high line, but it is sometimes advantageous to pronate (knuckles up) and slightly lower your foil hand in order to get below your opponent's foil arm.

Figure 10. *A Successful Low Line Attack*

Because of the smaller available target, attacks to the low line often land off target and will not count. But even when low attacks fail to hit, they may cause the opponent some anxiety. Most fencers are well-trained to defend against the more common high line attacks but are not as confident about protecting their low lines.

A creative fencer can combine various actions that we have previously discussed. For instance, disengagements can be done vertically by feinting to a high line and finishing to the low line or vice versa. Against an opponent who uses circle parries when you attack the high line, you can feint a straight thrust and do a partial double around the parry to finish in the outside low line. This not only avoids the circle parry but also the follow up lateral parry that a defender would likely make when he realizes that his circle parry was deceived.

26. *Low Line Defenses*

Parry Seven

The majority of attacks made against you will be made to one of your high lines, but you must learn to defend the low targets. The **parry seven** protects your inside low line, that is, the lower target near your left hip. As shown in figure 11, the foil hand is approximately where it would be for the parry four but the point is lowered to about knee level. The path taken by your foil to make this parry depends on where your foil hand was before the parry. If you were in the sixth position, the sequence would be to lower the point as you move your hand laterally to the left. If you were in the fourth position, the tip would follow an inward semi-circular path so as to meet the incoming blade and take it to the left. Do not pronate your hand while parrying seven. Your riposte can be directed to whatever target is open, either a high or a low line.

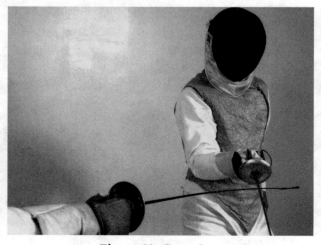

Figure 11. *Parry Seven*

The parry seven is also useful in blocking an opponent's attempt to feint to your inside high line and deceive your parry four. This is a risk you can take if you are fairly certain that your opponent will not make a direct attack to your inside high line. If all goes well, the disengaging blade will be stopped by your parry seven.

Parry Eight

This parry defends against attacks made to your outside low line, and as with the parry seven, your point will be at about knee level while your hand remains palm up and where it would be for a parry six. If you were in the fourth position before the parry, you will lower your point as you move your hand laterally to the right. From the sixth position, your tip will follow an inward semicircular path so as to meet and deflect the incoming blade to the right.

As described above for the parry seven, this parry can be used to block an opponent's attempt to disengage from your outside high line to the inside high line and can also be effective in stopping the final phase of a double. Thus the mind game goes on—a defender giving misinformation as to his real intentions, and an attacker trying to outwit attempts to parry.

Figure 12. *Parry Eight*

27. *Invitations*

It is not easy to score a touch on an opponent who maintains distance and parries effectively. As in a military operation, rather than attack the fort, it may be better strategy to fight the enemy outside the protective walls. So it is in fencing—you must try to get your opponent to come outside where you can spring an ambush.

An invitation is a defensive tactic in which the opponent is offered an opportunity to attack you without realizing that you have set a trap. Of the many possible invitations, the simplest is to purposely expose a target to tempt the opponent to attack so that you can parry and riposte. For example, if you assume an eighth position, your high line appears to be open to a direct attack that you are prepared to stop with a parry four or six. With the proper use of your fingers, a parry four or six from the eighth position can be incredibly fast.

An invitation can be so obvious that you are actually daring your opponent to lunge, in effect making him an offer he can't refuse; or it can be so subtle that the opponent does not recognize the potential trap. Finally, if you suddenly open a target while making a single rapid advance, your opponent might take the bait and make a reflexive lunge that you will easily parry.

As in all invitations, you must accurately judge your opponent's lunging length and speed, because it is pretty embarrassing to invite and then be hit. Taking any slightly exaggerated position can be useful; however, you can also invite with, for example, a point in line, because you know that your opponent will try to beat your blade and that you are fast enough to deceive the beat or to defend with a parry.

Another simple form of invitation is to make blade movements toward your opponent's foil as though trying to engage it. This could cause him to make a disengaging attack into your opening line, which you are prepared to defend. Anytime that you give an invitation, plan for unexpected reactions and always be ready to retreat if the attack is not what you are ready for. In fact, doing retreats repeatedly can also serve as an invitation for the opponent to do an advance lunge to catch up with you, and if you are sharp enough to detect when that will happen, you can hold your ground and parry.

28. Redoublements and Remises

These are not skills as such but rather are tactical. A **redoublement** is a renewal of an original attack that either missed or was parried by an opponent who failed to riposte. It is generally made while still in the lunge or after a forward recovery and involves a bending of the foil arm along with a blade movement to some open target. While you understand that a riposte has priority over a redoublement, some opponents are either slow to riposte or neglect to use their priority; in these cases you might use a renewed attack as a backup to your original attack. If needed, you can make several redoublements in succession, which becomes a matter of poke, poke, poke until you score. It may not be pretty, but sometimes you must resort to what will work. An aggressive, relentless fencer who makes strong attacks followed by redoublements may intimidate a timid or inexperienced fencer (not you of course). The answer is to learn to riposte immediately and to not let such fencers upset your composure.

A **remise** is defined as an attack that has been parried but continues on to hit the target without further effort by the attacking fencer. Remises and redoublements may both occur following attacks that were parried, but unlike a redoublement, a remise does not involve a new attempt to hit. It is very important to understand that neither a redoublement nor a remise has priority over an immediate simple riposte that hits either on or off target.

A remise is not generally a planned action, but it often results in a lucky touch for the attacker because the defender's riposte missed or was delayed. You can increase the likelihood of hitting with a remise by finishing your attacks with some **opposition,** which involves moving your hand slightly to the right or left during your lunge. By doing so, you are partially protecting your target during the final phase of your attack. Thus, if you are parried, the opponent will have some difficulty in making a direct riposte, and your remise might land after your attack was parried.

Using remises or redoublements should be secondary to having a well-planned and executed original attack. There has been serious consideration given to changing the rule regarding off-target touches. If such hits are viewed as misses and no longer cause a bout to stop, then we will see an increase in the use of redoublements and remises.

Conclusion

A lot of skills have been covered in this chapter. How well have you learned them? Be sure to spend the necessary time to perfect your skills and see appendix C for more drill ideas. But fencing is done as much with the head as with the blade, and the next chapter will show you more about how and when to use the skills that you now know. Also, now that you are doing more bouting, I suggest that you jump ahead to the end of chapter 8 and read a bit about some thoughts regarding fencing etiquette.

Self-Testing Questions

1. If you have your point in line, what can you expect an opponent to do about it?

2. Identify at least two uses for a beat.

3. Against what kind of attack might a beat parry be used most effectively?

4. What is a coupé and why would you choose to use it?

5. Which line does a parry eight defend?

6. In what sort of attack might a pronated hand be helpful?

7. Distinguish between a redoublement and a remise.

Strategies for the Intermediate Level Fencer

By this time you may have begun to develop a style of your own, one with which you are comfortable and have found to be somewhat effective. But there is always room for improvement in both skill execution and the use of tactics on the strip. In reality, a fencer never stops learning, and there is always a new strategy or a skill variation to try.

If your bout successes up to now have been the result of a technically sound game, you are fortunate and can build on it. But if you have been relying mainly on your natural athletic abilities, you can continue to develop only if you take time to work on technique and tactics. For the truly ambitious, there is no substitute for the guidance of a qualified fencing master. This sport requires constant study, and I tell my students that fencing is done from the neck up and all the rest is mechanical and conditioned responses.

Why is fencing sometimes referred to as physical chess? In that game you must analyze the pattern you see on the board and ask yourself such questions as: why did the opponent move a particular piece to a particular place? What should be my response, or is this a trap to be avoided? What might be the consequences, good or bad, if I then move a certain piece? In a fencing bout, there is precious little time to make similar decisions. Fencing is a miniature war, and information about the enemy is vital and must be quickly and correctly interpreted. Knowing what to do and when to do it is very important, but you also must have the skills and confidence to score the touch.

Strategy begins with analysis. You cannot solve a problem if you don't know what the problem is. Every time you are hit, identify how. Every time your attack fails, ask yourself why. Learn to read your opponent's body language because every movement can have some meaning if you are observant.

Once the basic skills have been learned well, the next step is to improve the mental process. Seek out and practice with a variety of fencers because you will stagnate if you always pair off with the same partner. When possible, try to fence with people who are just a bit more experienced or skilled than you are, because not much will be gained by always practicing with partners whom you can easily defeat.

Your club (*salle,* short for salle d'armes) is the place to perfect your skills to the point where you don't have to give them a second thought in a bout. The salle is your laboratory where you can conduct experiments, many of which will fail, but even in failing you should be learning something. I'm certainly not the first to say it, but you often learn more from losing a bout than from winning. You have to make a habit of analyzing what took place, how you were hit, how you scored touches, and what you might do the next time against that opponent. At the end of every practice bout, whether you won or you lost, if you did not learn anything about yourself or your opponent, then all you got out of it was some good exercise.

Be an interesting practice partner at your club. Instead of always trying to beat your teammate during a bout, occasionally present a problem to be solved such as fencing with a point in line or with an invitation. You might repeatedly use the same parry to encourage your partner to recognize what you are doing and make the appropriate deceiving attack. Thus, for short periods of time you are in effect acting the part of a coach.

If your club has electric scoring equipment, fence often using electric foils because the feel is a bit different than that of a "dry" foil, and the scoring box will clearly indicate whether or not you are touching (see chapter 9 on electric fencing). When no partner is available, practicing on a wall target of some sort can be very useful if you are attentive to detail regarding your form and accuracy. It allows you the luxury of being able to concentrate on improvement of the point control that is so vital in fencing.

The Role of Footwork in Tactics

Of course you learned to advance and retreat in your very first lesson, but do you really use your feet as part of your overall tactics or just as a means of transportation? Advancing is easy enough, and the only thing I would caution you about is that you should never take a step forward without being wary of a possible attack against you. Until you are ready to launch an attack, do not get within the opponent's lunging distance.

It is the retreat that I am most concerned about because many fencers seem to prefer to parry rather than give ground. The retreat is the single best defense against any attack, and of course it can be combined with parries. Note that a retreat can take the form of a rearward jump, which can be useful when you plan to immediately counter attack. A jump will store elastic potential energy in the leg muscles, and that energy can be instantly converted into the kinetic energy needed to lunge powerfully.

With every advance or retreat that you make, be ready to defend or attack. There is often only a brief instant in which you can make your unstoppable attack, and if you are not absolutely focused, it will come and go in a flash. Don't be casual, and be sure to always take short steps so that you can abruptly reverse your direction if needed. Make sudden changes in your footwork speed and direction if you think that doing so will confuse your opponent or gain some advantage for you. Try to acquire what I like to call clever feet to complement your clever hand. Being in control of the distance is the key element in successful fencing. Needless to say, your opponent is also trying to detect and take advantage of any lapse in your concentration. It is difficult to sustain a high state of vigilance through a bout, but this becomes easier as you acquire experience and self-confidence.

Some fencers bounce continually both while on guard and during footwork, somewhat like the movements of those who practice certain martial arts. That can be effective but is also very tiring if done for an entire bout. Just as when driving a stick-shift car you do not stay in the same gear for the whole trip, you should occasionally "change gears" in your footwork—sometimes slow, sometimes faster, and always unpredictable. If you typically move a lot during a bout, you might find that coming to a complete sudden stop may cause your opponent to wonder or worry momentarily about why you did so.

In some circumstances a retreat variation called a **pass** can be utilized. In doing a single rear pass, your front foot will cross behind the back foot, and you will resume an on guard stance. A series of rear passes, resembling a backward run, may be needed to get away from a rapidly advancing opponent. Maintaining good body position is vital. By yourself, practice blending a mixture of normal retreats and rear passes until you can do so smoothly and without tripping. A pass forward has no particular value.

Defense

Developing a sound defense is difficult and requires a lot of time and effort to become confident and proficient. Knowing *how* to parry isn't enough; you must also know *when* to parry, which parry to use, and when to retreat. It is possible to win a bout using only parries and ripostes, but the possession and use of a balanced game of attack and defense is essential.

Here is a list of some important defensive considerations for the fencer who already knows the mechanics of the various parries:

▶ Retreat more often than you parry so that your opponent will be forced to perhaps utilize an advance lunge, thus giving you more time to parry and riposte. But give ground reluctantly so as not to be run off the end of the strip and give your opponent an easy point. Retreating doesn't mean running away but, rather, methodically staying just out of distance so that you can stop whenever you are ready to parry and riposte.

▶ Regain ground at every opportunity so as to have ample room to retreat.

▶ Keep your distance against an aggressive opponent, and try not to be panicked into parrying.

▶ Be unpredictable in your defenses. Use a variety of parries in combination with retreats and an occasional point in line to give your opponent something to think about.

▶ Realistically, not every fencer uses conventional skills and tactics. The boxer versus the brawler has its fencing equivalent. It is very difficult to deal with an unskilled, aggressive opponent who charges down the strip leaving no time for you to develop a strategy. A crude fencer probably has not developed a solid defense, so I suggest that you make your own attack at the command to fence and not give the opponent a chance to do his thing.

▶ Develop your own set of perhaps three successive parries which will sweep a wide area and make it difficult for an aggressively advancing unpredictable opponent to find an easy opening to attack. Almost any combination will serve this purpose and should be perfected in practice. For example, try two circle sixes followed by a lateral four. Or lateral six, four, and six. Or four, circle four, and six. Or six, circle six, and four. In later chapters you will find other combinations that you might find effective in confusing an attacker and preventing a touch.

▶ When fencing someone who is effective at using beat attacks, keep your foil moving in some random but controlled manner so that it cannot be easily beaten. Or fence with your point below your hand level, perhaps in the eighth position, where it will not be vulnerable to a beat. That strategy is known as fencing with **absence of blade.**

▶ Try to frustrate your opponent by occasionally changing your blade position. For example, you can come on guard in fourth position instead of the usual sixth. That will allow you to use a circle parry four, which can be effective because it is uncommon and not always recognized by an attacker.

▶ You can stand on guard with a point in line, remove the line when you expect it to be attacked, and then replace it again. This repeated tactic could cause your opponent to become so preoccupied with finding a solution to the problem that you can attack unexpectedly with a good chance of scoring.

▶ A beat parry and riposte will effectively disrupt an attack being made by an opponent who is advancing with an extended arm feint.

▶ Position on the strip is often a factor in fencing and needs some study. There are fencers who prefer to hug one side of the strip, and you should not accommodate them. My advice to students is to fight from the opposite edge and perhaps entice the opponent to cross over to that less-preferred side. You may not get any additional touches by doing this, but your objective is to not let your opponent dictate where and how the bout will be fought. As for the end of the strip, of course you have to avoid stepping off.

▶ Now as to invitations, they are the most fun of any of the strategies. It is very difficult to touch an opponent who is on guard and ready to defend, so it is necessary to create openings. Tempt and dare your opponent to attack you; parry, riposte, and be pleased with your success while your opponent bemoans having been tricked. You do have to know your own abilities as well as those of your opponent. Of course an invitation will not always work, but when it does, it is very satisfying for you and upsetting for the opponent.

▶ If your direct ripostes are being parried, try one-two ripostes or aim for a low line target.

▶ Sometimes a delayed riposte can be more effective than an immediate one; be careful, however, that the opponent does not remise during your delay.

Offense

Needless to say, your opponent will do whatever it takes to stop your attempts to touch, and your offensive task is difficult if your opponent is on guard and prepared to parry or give ground. Therefore you have to be patient, look for patterns, and be ready to take advantage of your opponent's mistakes. If you can find the key to a door, it will be easier to open than if you try to break it down. Look for the key. You cannot solve a problem if you don't have a clear idea of what the problem is. Analyze and wait for opportunity.

If you have figured your chances of scoring with a certain attack are a lot better than fifty-fifty, your next task is to lunge at the proper time, which might, for example, be at the start of the opponent's advance or during the transition between his lunge and his recovery. Attacks that fail are usually due either to faulty execution or timing or to unexpected actions by the defender. It is imperative that you are always focused and are observant of every move of your opponent, who by the way is doing the same. There is no secret to success—just choose the right attack, use it at the right time, and deliver it with an unstoppable lunge. Sounds simple enough.

If you are unknowingly telegraphing your attacks, then of course your opponent will have time to defend or retreat. To avoid warning an opponent, never start an attack from a complete standstill. You can disguise the moment when you will attack by perhaps making a series of short forward movements of your torso, foil, or lead foot. Doing so might lull your opponent into not knowing which of those movements marks the start of a real attack.

There are two basic styles of attacking. One is a *premeditated* approach wherein, having observed certain patterns of parries being used by an opponent, you accordingly plan to feint and deceive the expected parries. I call the other method *opportunistic,* meaning that you simply advance under control while looking for an opening to attack. The first style is based on excellent analytic skills, while the second requires extremely quick reflexes and decision-making ability. A good fencer must be able to utilize either approach.

There is a solution to every problem, but first you have to identify the problem. Even when you know exactly what your opponent repeatedly does defensively, you must still determine whether you have the necessary skills to penetrate that defense. If you judge that you cannot score offensively, it may then be prudent to lure your opponent into attacking you so that you can perhaps defend and score with a riposte.

You must realize that there are many reasons why every attack you make will not land on target, and some of them may be out of your control. After all, your opponent does not want to be hit, and some unexpected action of his may cause your otherwise perfectly executed attack to miss. An inch one way or the other may be the difference between a valid hit and an off target touch.

Some additional things about offense to consider:

▶ Analyze, analyze, analyze. Show patience, patience, patience. Don't attack just to do something; have a reason for using that offensive skill at that time. But patience has limits when time is running out and you are behind in points. You may then have to take some offensive chances to avoid losing a bout due to time expiring.

▶ Always attack with the full expectation of scoring; no half-hearted lunges.

▶ Try to cultivate the habit of making an immediate parry four at the end of every lunge as a defensive backup in case your attack is parried. My reasoning is that most ripostes will most often be directed to your inside high line since that is the closest, largest, and most vulnerable target area. By somewhat automatically making a parry four at the end of every lunge, you gain a fraction of a second in defending over the time that would otherwise be needed to simply react to the opponent's parry and riposte.

▶   If your opponent parries well but ripostes either slowly or by compound actions, then by all means use redoublements or remises aimed at whatever target is open.

▶   The ability to make a quick recovery is important because your attacks will not always land, and you can often avoid a slow or delayed riposte by getting back on guard. If you are unable to recover quickly, you should remain in your lunge to parry.

▶   When you believe that your opponent will retreat from your lunge, you of course should use a very fast advance lunge along with the necessary blade action. In fact several advances may be required to catch up to a rapidly retreating fencer.

▶   If the opponent's usual response to your simple lunge is a short retreat, you may surprise her by unnoticeably bringing your rear foot quite close to your front foot before you lunge. This is sometimes referred to as a **gainer** lunge or an **inverse advance lunge** and can add many inches to the length of your lunge. A gainer lunge involves only two movements of the feet, whereas an advance lunge requires three. Each type has its place in offense.

▶   There are cool opponents who have good skills, don't react to feints, and are difficult for you to touch. Somehow you have to shake their confidence and take them "out of their game" as we say in sports. Your tactics of closing in while engaging and controlling their blades and perhaps forcing close quarters combat may rattle such fencers. Like a pit bull, keep the pressure on by not backing off. This may be a strategy of choice for the shorter fencer against a tall opponent who tries to use his reach advantage and stays at long range.

▶   The ability to step or jump back from an attack and then immediately counter-attack is a skill that you should develop because it is a very effective tactic. For just an instant, your opponent will be in transit between lunging and recovering and will perhaps be unprepared to defend against your surprise lunge or advance lunge.

▶ When you are unable to hit in the high line, try attacking the low line.

▶ When nothing you do offensively is working, stop attacking and see if your defense can get results. Remember the basic principle: if some tactic is not effective, then change.

▶ Be aware of the time remaining in the bout. Rules allow you to ask about the time only during normal breaks in the action. If you are trailing by a touch or two with only ten seconds left on the clock, you have to immediately go on the offensive. But if you are ahead on points and your opponent is not being aggressive, then you should let the clock run down.

▶ In a competition, concentrate only on the next touch and not the score. Never give up. Even if you are losing a bout by a 4–0 margin, try to get that next point because it may make a difference in your *seeding* to the next round. For the same reason, if you have a comfortable lead and know that you are going to win, don't give up a touch that could affect your seeding.

> ▶▶▶ Seeding from a pool into a direct elimination format is based primarily on your wins and losses but may also be determined by your *indicators*. These are found by subtracting the sum of all the touches scored against you (Touches Received) in the pool from the sum of all the touches that you made (Touches Scored) against all of your opponents (TS–TR). If you get a high seed, it means that your first direct elimination bout will be against a weaker

Before moving on to even more advanced skills, take a moment to assess where you are in terms of your offensive and defensive skills and your ability to apply them to your fencing. You already know enough by now to fence effectively for a long time without adding new skills.

Continue to cultivate the mental side of the sport so that you can deal with the wide variety of opponents you will encounter. Often, without realizing it, a person goes on the strip with the wrong frame of mind. For example, I have had students come to me with great anxiety that their next bout will be against a lefty and ask what they should do. They don't realize that no two lefties fence the same way, and there is no secret to fencing a left-hander. As with dealing with a right-hander, analyze the opponent and take appropriate action. My advice is to keep your foil, to the extent possible, on the outside of your opponent's so that you have a stronger parrying position. Make some of your ripostes from a parry four to a left-hander's low line, which by the way is what the lefty will be doing

Foil Action

to you. I often give lessons with my left hand to both right and left-handed students; after all, left-handers also have trouble fencing other left-handers.

Okay, if you are satisfied that you are ready to move up a level, then by all means read on! There is still more to be learned if you are to become a complete fencer.

▶ ▶ ▶ Have you ever wondered why anyone mounting a horse always does so from the left side? Does it matter to the horse? Perhaps the practice began centuries ago when knights and other armed warriors rode horseback. Visualize that you are wearing a sword of some type on your left side. Would it be easier or harder to mount from the right side of the horse? Would you really want to sling all that metal up and over the saddle? But the habit of left side mounting continues today even though swords are no longer worn. I have done a bit of riding and I now even get on my bicycle from the left side.

Advanced Skills

Perhaps you have skipped all the previous chapters because you are already beyond the beginner and intermediate levels. You must remember that effective fencing is not just a matter of having skills but involves using strategies as well. It might be a good idea for you to at least skim the earlier material where I may have included some tidbits of tactical information you can use. After all, skills are only tools and, by themselves, do not win bouts.

29. The Other Four Parries

So far I have covered parries four, six, seven, and eight, and you may have been wondering about missing parry numbers. What about one, two, three, and five? Let's start with and rule out parries three and five. **Parry three** is nothing more than a parry six but with the hand pronated (palm down) and it has very little use in foil fencing. The **parry five** is simply a low parry four and might be used instinctively when you begin to parry four and then realize at the last second that the attack is really being directed to your inside low line. Like the parry three it is seldom used on purpose.

The **parry two** does have utility and has the same function as the parry eight, that is, it defends the outside low line. To make this parry from the sixth position, make an inward-downward semi-circular blade movement to deflect the attacking blade. Instead of keeping the hand supinated as you would for the parry eight, pronate your hand and forearm (that is, turn the palm down). After the parry, your riposte will usually be to the opponent's high inside line, but you also have the option of riposting to the low line.

Why use parry two instead of eight? Well, it is stronger and can sweep a slightly wider area. One problem is that if it is deceived, a follow up parry is somewhat difficult. By comparison, eight is a weaker parry, but the foil hand is in a better position to make the transition to other parries if needed. So the choice is yours, and you should practice using both second and eighth parries.

The **parry one** is the strangest of the eight simple parries because it is a point down parry in which the foil hand moves laterally to the left and pronates. It has been said that the first position derives from where a sword would be when it is drawn from its scabbard. Parry one effectively protects the entire left side of your body, both high and low lines. The main problem with it is that a riposte is not easy for many fencers because of the awkward placement of the foil hand, and also because the foil tip is so far from the opponent's target. With some practice, however, it is possible to learn to riposte from a parry one, especially if you are using a pistol grip.

As you see in figure 13a, at the end of parry one, the foil hand and arm are no higher than your chin, the palm is facing away from you, and the point is at about knee level but well forward. If you expect to use this parry, it is a good idea to stand on guard in a second position, without being obvious about it, so that your hand will be already pronated and can more efficiently move to the parry.

For most fencers, the parries in descending order of importance and usefulness are four, circle six, six, eight, seven, two, one, five, and three. I would advise you to concentrate on perfecting the first four in that group. You should at least be familiar enough with all eight parries so that you can recognize any of them that might be used against you by some opponent.

Figure 13a. *Parry One*   **Figure 13b.** *Parry Two*

30. The Flèche

By definition, a **flèche** (pronounced *flesh*) is any attack in which the rear leg crosses the front leg. On the one hand it is not an essential skill, but there are times when it can be used to reach someone who maintains good distance or who might be surprised by its use. Shorter fencers might find a need to use the flèche more than would a taller fencer.

One way to start learning to flèche is by pairing with a partner who is positioned closer than lunge distance but farther than a simple thrust distance. Extend your foil arm and lean well forward from your on guard position to touch the target partner, *without moving either of your feet*. You should feel as though you will fall since your weight is now over your right foot. This lean must be made both with a forward movement of your hips as well as of your shoulders. Next, your partner should move slightly farther back so that as you again lean, you will be so off balance that you must bring your left leg forward to prevent a fall. Your right foot should not move. Finally, the partner will stand just beyond your lunge distance, and you will extend, lean, and bring your rear leg forward, all in a continuous, fluid movement, and land your touch. There will usually be a few running steps following the touch, partly to allow you to slow your momentum gradually, rather than abruptly, and partly to take you out of riposte distance should the attack be parried.

The power for the flèche comes from the extension of the front leg. In some instances a flèching fencer may even be momentarily airborne, a projectile as it were. In French, flèche means arrow, which is descriptive of how fast your foil should move to the target—straight and fast. Of the various ways to do a flèche,

Figure 14. *The Flèche*

the poorest is to start from a conventional on guard stance because the center of gravity is too centered to allow for an explosive attack. Knowing that you will be flèching, you should shift your weight slightly forward in your on guard position and assume a fairly deep crouch.

Another way to initiate a flèche is to do it immediately following a half lunge hoping to lull your opponent into thinking that your half lunge indicates the end of your attack. A final method is to jump back out of reach of an attack and then flèche to counter-attack. In jumping back, you should end with the front foot directly under your center of gravity so that you can take off like a sprinter out of the "starting blocks." But remember that a flèche is not a running attack; you should not run down the strip in pursuit of the opponent. Your touch should land at about the same time that the rear leg crosses over and seldom any later than that. A flèche is just another delivery method and any of your blade skills may be used to deceive possible parries.

> ▶▶▶ **Force is a vector quantity, which means that it has both a magnitude and a direction. In the flèche, the direction of the front leg's force application should be as horizontal as possible for maximum effect. This explains why it is necessary to have a slight forward lean before launching your attack; your center of gravity will be more in line with the leg's horizontal force component. Vertical motion should be minimized.**
>
> **Center of gravity is a point at which all of a body's weight is concentrated, a balance point so to speak. It is not a fixed point and varies as a body's position changes.**

Now I have already said that the flèche is not essential in foil (it is illegal in saber), but I must also add that it is potentially dangerous because of the tremendous force involved. If by chance both fencers decide to flèche at the same moment, one or both could be injured if they happen to collide. And a worse result might be expected if the flèche is made with a stiff, unyielding arm that could result in blade breakage with possible penetration of an opponent's uniform or mask. If you must flèche, be sure to veer off to one side or another so as to avoid collision. Until you have achieved the ability to touch lightly and with absolute control in practice, **do not flèche!**

If faced with an opponent who often uses the flèche, you can of course use whatever parry is appropriate, or you can maintain a slightly longer than usual distance so that you have more time to detect and defend the attack. Another strategy is to stay on the edge of one of the side boundaries of the strip to cut off whichever path seems to be preferred by the attacker.

31. *Attacking an Opponent's Blade*

Other than using a beat as described in chapter 5, there are other options available for attacking a blade, but most have limited use. There is a French term, **prise de fer,** which basically refers to any action that controls and diverts an opponent's blade during an attempt to score a touch.

The **bind** is one of several types of prises de fer. It generally is useful only against a point in line and, as the name implies, it is supposed to tie up and move aside the threatening blade. A bind is difficult to illustrate, so try to visualize my description. Your partner will stand at lunge distance with his point in line and aimed at your chest. Starting from a sixth position, engage the partner's blade in fourth with the strong middle or near third (the forte) of your blade contacting the weak end (the foible) of your partner's. Lower your point onto the side opposite to that of the engagement; and then lunge while also moving your hand to the right.

The desired result is to land a touch while controlling and moving the threatening blade off to your right where it won't touch you. The most common error is making a large, telegraphed bind. Done correctly, the tip of your foil should be moving directly forward as soon as contact has been made with the opponent's blade. Be sure to keep your foil hand at about shoulder height throughout the bind, and do not pronate your hand. In a bout you won't have a cooperative partner, and there are so few opportunities to use a bind in foil fencing that I seldom take the time to teach it to any but advanced fencers.

Other forms of prises de fer, such as the glide, graze, and pressure, are only occasionally useful and then only in very specific scenarios. One which I do teach is the **cross** (croisé) which has some similarity to the bind but is used primarily in riposting. It is best done following a parry six against a left-handed fencer. As the parry six is completed, lower your hand and foil point while also extending to hit the opponent's outside low line. You must maintain continuous control while forcing the opposing blade away from your target. The cross may be a good choice if you are having difficulty in touching with a direct riposte or when your opponent is effectively remising after you have parried. Unlike in a bind, the foil hand during the cross stays on the same side as the parry.

32. *Defending Against a Bind*

If you have your point in line and are facing an opponent who is more likely to bind than to beat, you could try to *deceive* the bind and thereby retain your priority. This must be done mostly by use of the fingers so that your foil tip will be moved just enough to avoid the bind. A large deceptive action could result in loss of priority. Of course your arm must remain straight throughout, and your intent is not just to deceive but to touch the attacker. This is a very difficult skill and should be tried only against opponents who make slow or telegraphed bind attempts.

You could also choose to *resist* the bind by stiffening your elbow and grip. Doing so serves the same purpose as a parry, and you will then try to hit with a riposte. And finally, you could use the beautiful **yielding parry** in which your presumably well-trained hand senses the force of the bind and, instead of resisting, allows the attacker's bind to literally guide your blade to a parry four. Blade contact must not be lost as your yielding blade sort of pivots around the incoming blade. You will riposte following your parry. Resisting bind attempts is somewhat natural, whereas the yielding parry requires considerable skill.

33. *The Flick*

The **flick** is a variation of the cutover and is sometimes derisively compared to fly-casting because it involves a whip like action that usually touches high on the shoulder or even on the back of an opponent. It has been a source of controversy between young, athletic fencers and older, more traditional purists who lament that the flick should never have of right of way. There is no doubt that, in the hands of a skilled fencer, the flick is very effective both as an attack and as a riposte. It requires the use of a flexible foil blade, a pistol grip, and a strong wrist.

The flick begins with an elevation of the foil hand while also bending the elbow somewhat in the manner of an exaggerated cutover. Next, the elbow starts to extend and the wrist begins its forward fly-cast motion followed by an abrupt stop, which allows the blade's flexibility to continue the tip's downward arc toward the intended target. A flick can also be used to riposte following either a lateral parry four or a circle parry six, and is most effective when the entire parry-flick sequence is done without any interruption.

Defense against a flick is difficult and usually involves the raising of your hand to a diagonally high sixth parry to block the incoming blade. Alternatively, you can take a step forward to cause the flick to land flat on your shoulder (ouch!). The first of these may be a reflexive act while the other is premeditated and accompanied by an attempt to touch.

Because of new modifications to scoring machines that became effective in late 2004, flicks are being used much less often in competition. The time of contact needed between the foil tip and the target was increased, and that change favors the use of thrusting actions over the quick light flicks that many foilists have depended upon.

34. *Stop Hit*

A **stop hit** is a risky tactic that is often used incorrectly and reflexively. It is nothing more than a well-timed thrust into an opponent's complex or delayed preparatory action. To expect a referee to award the stop hit touch to you, you must actually hit *before* the *start* of the opponent's final movement, that is, before the priority-gaining action begins. This is a judgment call by the referee, and your action must be so clearly correct that the call will favor you rather than the attacker. My advice to beginning and intermediate level fencers is to use parries rather than stop hits. When you find that your opponent relies a lot on stop hits, make direct attacks which always have priority over stop hits.

There is a variation of the stop hit whereby the defender reaches forward to land a touch, usually into a preparation, and immediately moves out of distance of the attack. Simultaneously with the touch attempt, the back leg is stretched well back in position for a quick rear recovery. To use this tactic successfully requires good anticipation, timing, and quickness, and it helps to have long arms. The intent is to touch and *not be touched*, whereas when a stop hit is used the defender may be hit but hopes that she had priority.

Figure 15. *A Stop Hit by the Fencer on the Left*

35. *Infighting*

At close quarters there is no right of way, and usually the first person to hit gets the point. As a referee I normally allow two fencers to infight as long as rules are being obeyed and there is no impasse. Getting close together is often unintended, but there are fencers who relish infighting and purposely close in. Body contact, called **corps-à-corps**, must be avoided because it will result in a warning from the referee.

I do spend time teaching students the basic principles of close fighting because the situation arises often enough that a fencer must know what to do. Consider the following:

▶   As soon as you find yourself close to your opponent, you must instantly assess which, if either, of you has an advantageous blade position. If you do, then try to hit, usually by first pulling your arm well back so as to be able to clear your foil (after all it is 35 inches long) to where it can touch the opponent. It is often necessary to step to the side with your leading foot to give you a better angle from which to thrust.

▶   If you do not have a favorable blade position, then by all means try to tie up the opponent's blade so that it cannot touch you. Generally, the referee will call a halt rather quickly.

▶   Once you are in close, never back out because you will be more vulnerable to being hit. If you find yourself at a distinct disadvantage, it is permissible to move past your opponent, and the bout will be stopped due to the reversal of positions.

There are no specific drills to improve infighting skills. Work with a willing partner and assume many different blade configurations from which you both attempt to hit or try to prevent being hit. Some fencers will twist, duck, or even jump in an effort to score. Just remember that body contact, turning the back to the opponent, and covering target with the rear arm are forbidden.

36. *Second Intention*

This really is not a new skill as such but rather is a tactic utilizing some skills that you already know. It takes many forms and is used against opponents who have somewhat predictable but effective responses to certain of your actions. For example, if faced with a fencer who has a very good direct riposte and whose parries you are having trouble deceiving, you can make a realistic half lunge that you expect will be parried (your first intention). Your second intention is to parry the riposte and make your own counter-riposte. The use of a half-lunge allows you to have the time and space to successfully parry the opponent's fast riposte.

Your counter-riposte may not be able to reach the target from the half-lunge position, so you should complete the action by moving your lead foot forward into a full lunge.

There are many possible variations of second intention patterns, and the one just described is a simple, but useful example. Most forms share the concept of making some initial action that draws a response by the opponent that the attacker hopes to be able to act upon.

Some Concluding Notes

Most of the common foil blade skills have now been covered, but a good fencer does not need to use, or even to know, every possible skill. Concentrate on being able to perform a few skills really well and at the right time. I have not touched on some body actions such as ducking or twisting the torso to avoid being hit. Agile fencers in specific situations could certainly use these, but my suggestion is that you focus on perfecting basic skills before you experiment with body evasion tactics.

Self-Testing Questions

1. Name two parries in which the hand is pronated.

2. Which parry defends both the high and low inside line?

3. What fencing action can be called "the arrow"?

4. Define "prise de fer."

5. What is the name for body contact?

6. Why is it risky to rely on using the stop hit?

7. In a second intention attack, what is the "first intention"?

Getting Your Point Across

I define tactics or strategies as being the creative and appropriate use of distance and blade skills, both offensively and defensively. Of course, the effectiveness of any plan of action depends on proper timing and positive execution. It is important to not only know *what* to do but you must also know *when* to act and to have the ability to perform the skill. Study and training as well as a lot of bout experience are needed to achieve a high level of tactical competence. Other key ingredients include excellent physical condition and a willingness to fight.

Now for a disclaimer. Much of what has been covered in previous chapters is what I will call academic. In the real world of competitive fencing, most of the skills you have learned so far just cannot be easily used against high-rated opponents. For the beginning or recreational fencer, the varieties of skills described in earlier chapters are fun to learn, help to demonstrate the complexity of the sport, and stimulate the thinking process. But now as an advanced fencer, you should rely more and more on selecting the simplest skill to use at just the right moment with speed and precision.

At this level, the actions are so fast that a phrase seldom goes beyond one counter riposte before a touch is scored. Opponents will not react as easily to your feints or invitations. None of this is meant to say that you have wasted your time in learning useless skills. The more that you know, the better. It's like having a well-stocked toolbox containing some tools that you use regularly and some that you might need only once a year (I own tools that I've never used).

You must develop the habit of analyzing your opponent before, during, and after a bout because you might have to fence that person again later. This ability takes time to perfect and requires some concentrated observation. Closely watch your future opponents. What did this fencer do in winning earlier bouts or how did his opponents score their touches? If you can come onto the strip with at least a little bit of information on which to base your strategy, you will be better prepared. Success in any battle relies upon getting information about the enemy, giving misinformation, and withholding information. Even the wisest general (your mind) can win only if the troops (your legs and blade skills) are up to the task.

If you had no opportunity to scout your opponent beforehand, you should start the bout with a couple of half-lunges to see what, if any, reaction you get. But whenever you make such probing actions, you must be alert to a counter attack.

A pool bout is a short three minutes long, so there is no time to waste waiting for just the right conditions before you attack, especially if you are behind in the score. Identify weaknesses in your opponent's defense and have the courage to execute the correct action to score. During, and even before a bout, assess the opponent's offensive capabilities in terms of her speed, skill, and lunge length, so that you can devise some means of neutralizing her strong points. These abilities to identify and assess are keys to becoming a successful fencer.

> ▶▶▶ The often-quoted Prussian general, Karl Von Clausewitz (1780–1831) made observations that have implications for fencers including:
>
> "War is nothing but a duel on an extensive scale." (Can I paraphrase that by saying a fencing bout is a miniature war?)
>
> "Nothing is accomplished in warfare without daring . . . we cannot be readily ruined by a single error, if we have made reasonable preparations."
>
> "The best form of defense is attack."
>
> "Courage, above all things, is the first quality of a warrior."
>
> "It is even better to act quickly and err then to hesitate until the time of action is past."

Taking Charge

With experience, you will learn to be in command of a bout, and that process starts from the moment you step onto the strip. Your behavior and body language must convey to the opponent your self-confidence and expectation of winning, even as you may be trembling with doubts. When the referee says "on guard," "ready?" answer with a clear "Yes!" Your confident response may send a message to your opponent that you are indeed ready to fence. But any such pre-bout psychology goes only so far, and you still need the skills and tactics to win.

While skills and tactics are vital, there is much more to being a consistently effective fencer. Your abilities to focus, to take advantage of opportunity, and to refuse to be dominated are intangibles that can't always be coached. **Be the puppeteer, not the puppet.** Always try to take away your opponent's favorite game as if to say, "Hey, we are playing by *my* rules."

Some Thoughts about Defense

▶ You probably have a favorite blade position from which to attack or defend, but if that is not working, then try assuming another position. For example, coming on guard in a slightly higher sixth position may be effective in discouraging an opponent's flicks or cutovers. Being in a fourth position is somewhat unusual, could serve as an invitation, could momentarily confuse your opponent, and could give you the capability of using a circle parry four against an attack to your high outside line.

▶ Having your point in line will force an aggressive opponent to pause and think about what to do to remove your treat.

▶ An eighth position will place your blade out of danger against a fencer whose game depends on using beats or pris de fer attacks, while at the same time it can serve as an invitation or as a different place from which to launch an attack. Every position you might assume can have both an offensive and defensive value, but you must practice enough to be comfortable and skilled with what you choose.

▶ The essence of defense is *unpredictability,* but close behind is the ability and willingness to maintain your preferred distance. You must learn to rely on retreating from attacks while patiently awaiting the right time to parry and riposte. By doing so, you also create opportunities to step forward and touch your opponent on his preparatory advances which he makes with the expectation that you will again retreat. Although this may be considered an offensive tactic, it follows from defensive retreats designed to give the opponent misinformation and disturb his confidence.

▶ If your opponent is very aggressive and forces you to retreat, do so while also using a combination of several varied parries to make it difficult for the attacker to find an opening to hit. Alternatively, you can try to make your own attack at the instant of the command to fence, thereby forcing the opponent to defend.

▶ Attacking into preparation is risky because if both fencers touch, the referee will likely rule in favor of the attacker. When closing into an opponent's preparation, try to not only touch but also to divert the incoming blade by blocking the threatened line with a pris de fer action so as to avoid a double touch. The trick is to correctly anticipate and time the opponent's preparation.

▶ If you elect to parry, do so at the very onset of the attack before it has had a chance to develop. In other words, go after the feint with a *beat parry*. Such early interception of the incoming blade is not always possible, so the next best strategy is to retreat, ignore the opponent's feints, and parry only the final action.

▶ The low line parries, especially seven and eight, tend to be under-used but can be very effective in blocking attempts by an opponent who often utilizes successive one-two attacks or doubles. Try to mislead your opponent into thinking that you will use lateral parries. Then if you can sense the moment that she is likely to try to deceive your parries, you can simply lower your tip to either a parry seven or eight to block the passage of the incoming blade under your hand. Of course if your tactic is successful, you must riposte to whatever target is open.

▶ Direct ripostes from a parry four can be done two ways. One is to use **opposition** by moving your tip in a straight line from the parry to the target thereby keeping your inside line somewhat closed to oppose the attacker's remise or counter-riposte. The other choice is to riposte by moving your foil hand to the right thus using sixth opposition, *whether or not you actually make contact* with the attacking blade. This will close your outside line in case your parry attempt is deceived by a disengagement. My reasoning for this tactic is that, even if you failed to parry, your extension with opposition may block the blade that successfully deceived you or may cause it to hit your arm.

▶ Similarly, you can sometimes get away with an immediate riposte from a parry two, again whether or not contact was made. If you stand on guard in sixth with your foil hand slightly higher than normal, you can use the parry two to sweep a wide area and defend against attacks made to either your low or high line. The parry two is correctly made by pronating your foil hand to parry and then supinating it to riposte to the high line. I call this a *roll-unroll* action because you would roll your hand a quarter turn to pronation and then unroll it to riposte, all the while keeping your hand high and to the outside so as to block any deception of your parry. To reduce point travel, your forearm and blade should be in a fairly straight line during both the parry and the riposte. Alternatively, the riposte from two can be directed to the opponent's low line.

▶ A circle parry six should always be a surprise to your opponent. An immediate riposte can follow even if you failed to make contact because you should have no reason to think that a double will even be attempted. This assumes that you have not shown any predictable patterns of parries and that you are not so obvious in doing your circle six that an experienced opponent would be able to make a double around it. Note that the circle six parry can also be done while simultaneously extending the arm thereby combining the parry and riposte in a single tempo.

▶ While I don't advocate it, some agile fencers can effectively duck (*passata soto*) or side step (*inquartata*) to avoid attacks while also trying to score touches. Such displacing moves go back centuries and require a lot of practice to learn to properly sense the right moment to act. When you fence someone who uses such tactics, it is advisable to make some realistic initial false action to cause the opponent to prematurely try to evade and thus become vulnerable to your final attack.

More Thoughts about Offense

Defensive skills are much more difficult to learn and depend upon than are offensive skills, so unless you have a superb defense, you should attack more often than do your opponents. The attack always has the advantage for several reasons. The possible outcomes of an attack are:

▶ There was a touch, perhaps even a lucky touch.

▶ The attack hit off target, which stops the bout.

▶ The attack missed.

▶ The attack was parried.

Three of those four actions were failures, but that does not mean much if you as the attacker were not hit. Your failed attack could perhaps be followed by your redoublement if the opponent is slow to counter attack. The parried attack may be followed by the opponent's riposte which itself might miss, hit you off target, or be parried by you.

The math favors the attack, but there are several principles to keep in mind:

▶ Patience. Do not attack just to be doing something. The right move at the right time is your objective, but the right moment does not always just pop up. You may have to create it by subtly planting ideas in your opponent's head as to what he has to do defensively. It is difficult, but you must read your opponent's mind as to what he is likely to do next or what he thinks you are likely to do. But don't forget that all the while he is trying to figure you out as well—ah, athletic chess. Remember the principle that applies in most sports: if whatever you are doing is working, do not change, but if your tactics are failing, then try another approach.

▶ Very often an attack fails to reach because the opponent retreated. A lot of energy is wasted chasing an opponent down the strip. **If you want to catch someone, *back up*.** Your step back may prompt the opponent to step forward to stay in distance. If you can start your attack at the very moment of that advance your opponent will not have time to reverse direction.

▶ A form of opportunistic style that works well for some naturally aggressive fencers involves a determined but seemingly out of control series of advances with the foil moving through random threatening patterns. There are many variations of this tactic, but they all involve putting pressure on an opponent, causing her to retreat, perhaps in panic. All the while the advancing fencer is looking for an opening to attack. The advancer might extend to various lines and withdraw her foil repeatedly to confuse the retreating defender or to cause her to attempt a poorly timed stop hit. This relentless marching style is certainly not pretty to watch but it can be effective, particularly when other tactics have not been getting results. It does put a burden on the referee to determine priority if both fencers score, but there is a tendency to favor the attacker unless the defender clearly establishes an early line or manages a correct stop hit.

▶ In what has been termed a **modern disengage** attack, a feint is made in the usual way, but instead of retaining an extended arm while deceiving the parry, the arm is flexed. Thus, the foil is withdrawn to avoid the parry and the arm re-extended immediately to touch in the newly opened line. The advantage of this method is that it can be used against either lateral or circular parries, and the withdrawal can even be held a bit if a series of consecutive parries are to be deceived.

▶ The use of an occasional shout with your attack may serve to unnerve an opponent, but it can also be useful in giving you a boost when you are feeling sluggish. It is sometimes done with the hope of influencing the referee's decision regarding priority. Do not overdo it because it will lose any effectiveness and, more importantly, can become obnoxious, as is too often the case when fencers attack with what can only be described as screams.

▶ Consider attacking your opponent's low line occasionally because most fencers are not as adept at defending that area. You can for instance feint to the high line to draw a lateral parry and terminate in the low line. Once you have scored with a low touch, the opponent may become anxious about future attacks there, and your feint to the low target may draw a low parry and thus open a high line to your attack.

▶ You should use the very effective tactic of stepping or jumping back out of reach of an attack and then launching a quick counter attack with an appropriate blade skill. During the brief transition from lunge completion to recovery, there is just an instant where the attacker is vulnerable to a counter action. You may find this tactic being used against you and, if so, you can utilize a second intention action such as making a deliberately short lunge and then being set to parry the expected counter attack.

▶ There is a variation of the lunge that I call, for lack of another name, the **long step.** This is nothing more than the usual lunge followed instantly by a forward recovery. It can be useful when you are not sure whether your opponent will retreat or stand still when you attack. You try to hit with the original attack, but if your opponent retreats, you will already be in position to lunge a second time.

Other Considerations

When competing, you must pay attention to the referee's description of actions and how right of way is being called. In local meets, there can be a wide range of officiating quality and a wise fencer will try to adjust his game to satisfy a particular referee's interpretation of priority. Even when you are right, it is a waste of energy to argue with the decisions. At any level, officiating is difficult, and you should show respect to these mostly volunteer referees who do the best they can. Good sportsmanship reflects favorably on you and your coach. You need to have a thorough knowledge of the rules so that if the referee is misapplying a rule, you can politely so state or even request a ruling by the bout committee.

In your free time, think about various scenarios that you might expect to encounter so that when the occasion arises during a bout, you will already have thought through your course of action. For example, think about what you should do in situations where there are just a few seconds left and you are leading by some score or your opponent is in the lead. Should you retreat to run out the clock? What is your opponent likely to do in the same situation? I believe that such mental practice can make a major contribution to your total game.

On the strip you may find that your opponent seems to anticipate every attack you make, probably because you are telegraphing the start of the action. It is difficult during a bout to correct this signaling of your attacks, but you can at least disguise your movements by deliberately sending false messages so that the defender cannot identify when the real attack is coming. For example, before lunging you might move your upper body forward and backward a few times and perhaps add some blade actions and very short leading foot movements. Giving such misinformation is important but would not even be necessary if your attacks were always correctly delivered without warning.

During direct elimination bouts, there is a one-minute break after three minutes of fencing time and another at the end of the second round of three minutes. A coach or teammate may give you advice while you rest or take a drink of water. This minute of discussion can certainly make a difference in the bout's outcome, so don't waste it. Remember that your opponent may very well be using the time to figure out how to deal with you, so be cautious during the first few seconds of the bout's resumption. No matter what the score, do not let up because the concept of momentum change is very real. You can come back to win even when trailing by several points, but then so can your opponent. The bout isn't over until it's over.

Sometimes skill training teaches a fencer to respond so automatically to certain actions of an opponent that it takes real effort to "override" what has been so thoroughly learned. For instance, if you always make a direct riposte following a parry four, you might recognize that your opponent is parrying your ripostes and that you may need to use a one-two. But it may be hard to break your habit of direct riposte. You must be adaptable in both the offensive and defensive aspects of your game.

I mentioned earlier that rules change from time to time and it is very important to stay aware of these even when they are only in the discussion or experimental stages. For example, there has been talk about eliminating the white light resulting from an off target hit in foil fencing. This is something I have advocated for many years and it may yet come to pass. The advantages include speeding up competitions, making the sport easier for spectators to follow, eliminating the need for costly metallic strips, and not rewarding a fencer whose inaccuracy prevents a riposte or counter attack. With the white light removed, it might make wireless foil fencing bouts possible. If that rule change were to be adopted, it would require a major change in a fencer's tactics, and some would say that foil will become épée with a smaller target. However, the priority rule would remain as is to continue to differentiate foil from épée.

> ▶ ▶ ▶ **Many years ago, a "no foul" rule was tried with success in Big Ten Conference meets and for one year in the NCAA championships before the adoption of the electric foil. The trials produced favorable results but were discontinued probably because the collegiate fencers had to make adjustments when competing in non-collegiate or international meets which continued to recognize off target touches.**

Sound technical skills, good footwork, and a reasonable understanding of tactics are all very important. But there are some intangibles that cannot be taught and at any skill level they often make the difference between winning and losing. Everyone wants to win, but some seem to want to win more than others. We have all seen fencers who have just lost a bout but don't seem to be bothered by it, and we have seen others who become quite upset at the loss. Some athletes simply hate losing so much that they are driven to fight harder and find the energy to come from behind while others seemingly give up. The psychology of sports is a fascinating field of study.

There is a lot to be said for the recreational fencer who simply enjoys the sport and is concerned not so much with winning practice bouts as with having fun and exercise. But if you are a competitive fencer, of course winning is important. At the end of a bout that did not end favorably, ask yourself this question: Did my opponent win or did I lose? If your opponent was clearly better than you, then he won and you can accept that. However, if you did not fence well, had no focus, missed opportunities, and were not thinking, then you lost and that should be incentive enough to make you work even harder to improve.

Etiquette

▶ ▶ ▶ In many professional sports we see showboating, poor sportsmanship, fighting, and also bad fan behavior. Fencing should be above all of that because it takes away from the long traditions of the sport. Coaches and referees must take the lead in teaching and enforcing standards of acceptable behavior. After all, it is only a game. There is more to life than fencing, but fencing does add something to life. Like it or not, you will be judged by your strip behavior, and I hope that you will never have the reputation of being ill-tempered or a bad sport.

I need to describe one of the greatest acts of sportsmanship ever recorded in sports. In the 1928 Olympic Games, naval Lt. George Calnan lost a likely gold medal in épée when he acknowledged a hit against himself that the judges had not seen. Clearly he was an officer and a gentleman. He fenced in four Olympics and was given the honor of taking the Olympic oath on behalf of all the athletes at the '32 games in Los Angeles.

Electric Foils and Competition Procedures

I f you now have reached some level of competency with the foil but have not yet fenced with the electric foil, this chapter is for you. Electric foil scoring equipment has been in use since the mid-1950s, some twenty or so years after the épée had gone electric. It took longer to develop the electric foil apparatus because it had to be able to distinguish between on-target and off-target touches. Such equipment was necessitated by the inconsistencies of visual judging and the occasional concern about cheating by judges. You will enjoy electric fencing even more than "dry" fencing because it removes doubts about whether or not there was a touch.

▶▶▶ Electric foil tips have changed over the years. Originally they had sharp prongs which soon were determined to be too dangerous. Then rounded tips with concentric circular ridges were tried briefly around 1961 before, finally, the current flat tip was approved.

What Happens at a Competition?

When you arrive at the meet site to register and pay your entry fee, you might have to present your mask to be inspected and punch-tested. Masks have to resist penetration by the test device and have to be free of obvious defects or rust. Meanwhile, the meet organizers will be preparing pool sheets, which is usually done by computer programs based on fencers' seedings, and you will soon know when you will be fencing and against whom.

Note that the completed pool sheet example (figure 16) shows that only four competitors were entered, each of

Date: _____

Event: _____

Pool # _____

Indicators (1999 FIE/USFA Rules; o.19)
1st:V/B   2nd:HG-HT   3rd:HG

	1	2	3	4	5	6	7	8	# Vict	Indic. (V/B)	Hits Given	Hits Taken	Indic. (Hg - Ht)	Rank
1		~~IIII~~ V	~~IIII~~ V	~~IIII~~ V					3		15	6	+9	1
2	II / 2		~~IIII~~ V	III / 3					1		10	14	-4	3
3	IIII / 4	IIII / 4		~~IIII~~ V					1		13	12	+1	2
4	O / O	~~IIII~~ V	II / 2						1		7	13	-6	4
5														
6														
7														
8														

Bout Order
Number of Fencers:

3	4	5	6	7		8	
3 bouts	6 bouts	10 bouts	15 bouts	21 bouts		28 bouts	
1-2	1-4	1-2	1-2	1-4	1-6	2-3	3-6
2-3	2-3	3-4	4-5	2-5	2-4	1-5	2-8
3-1	1-3	5-1	2-3	3-6	7-3	7-4	5-4
	2-4	2-3	5-6	7-1	6-5	6-8	6-1
	3-4	5-4	3-1	5-4	1-2	1-2	3-7
	1-2	1-3	6-4	2-3	4-7	3-4	4-8
		2-5	2-5	6-7		5-6	2-6
		4-1	1-4	5-1		8-7	3-5
		3-5	5-3	4-3		4-1	1-7
		4-2	1-6	6-2		5-2	4-6
			4-2	5-7		8-3	8-5
			3-6	3-1		6-7	7-2
			5-1	4-6		4-2	1-3
			3-4	7-2		8-1	
			6-2	3-5		7-5	

Indicators
(Bouts top, Victories left)

	2	3	4	5	6	7
0	0.000	0.000	0.000	0.000	0.000	0.000
1	0.500	0.333	0.250	0.200	0.167	0.143
2	1.000	0.667	0.500	0.400	0.333	0.286
3		1.000	0.750	0.600	0.500	0.429
4			1.000	0.800	0.667	0.571
5				1.000	0.833	0.714
6					1.000	0.857
7						1.000

Fencers

1 JONES _____

2 SMITH _____

3 RAMIREZ _____

4 BENSON _____

5 _____

6 _____

7 _____

8 _____

Figure 16. *A Round Robin Pool Sheet*

whom has fenced the other three. Such a format is known as a **round robin.** Pool bouts are fought for five touches to win or for three minutes, whichever comes first. The scorekeeper has entered the results of the bouts and it is clear that Jones came in first with three wins and no losses. The other fencers each won one bout and lost two thereby being in a tie. The final placements were determined by the **indicators** for each fencer as calculated by subtracting the total touches received from the total touches scored (TS–TR). Ramirez scored thirteen touches and was hit twelve times for a plus one indicator that was good for second place. Smith scored ten total touches and subtracting the fourteen scored against her resulted in a minus four indicator to earn third place ahead of Benson who had a minus five.

You should know that your margins of victory or loss in the pool are factored into determining your seeding into the next round that might again be pools or, more commonly, **direct elimination,** or DE. In the DE format fifteen touches are needed to win within a nine-minute time limit. That time is divided into three rounds of three minutes each with a one minute break in between. As the name implies, if you lose a DE bout you are done for the day, but if you advance, you will face increasingly stronger opponents in each succeeding bout.

When the scorekeeper calls out the names of the fencers for a bout, the one whose name is called first will get on the strip to the right of the referee. If one of the two fencers is left-handed, that person always goes to the left side (unless the opponent is also a lefty).

The next step is to plug one end of your body cord into the reel socket and the other into your foil socket. Be sure that your body cord's alligator clip is attached to the back of your lamé on your *foil arm side* as required by the rules.

The referee will then place a 500 gm weight on the tip of your vertically held foil and will give it a tap to activate the white light on the scoring box. In order to pass this test, your foil's tip spring must be strong enough to lift the weight back up and thereby cancel the white light. If it fails to do so, you will receive a yellow warning card which stays in effect through that bout, and of course you will need to replace it with your second foil. If by chance that one also fails, you get a red card which means that your opponent will get a point even before the bout has started. You can see that it pays to thoroughly check your mask, body cords, and foils before you go to the meet. Between bouts you can do a temporary fix of a weak spring by taking it out and stretching it a bit.

The last test is done by touching your opponent's lamé with your foil tip to see if the colored light on your side turns on, and if it does, you then stand behind the on guard line and salute your opponent and the referee. The commands of the referee are "On guard," "Ready?" "Fence" and the bout starts. If one fencer touches the other, either on or off the target, the referee will call a halt to the bout and determine priority before awarding any valid hit. The fencers will go back to the on guard lines if a point was awarded, otherwise the fencers resume fencing from their positions at the time the halt was called.

> ▶▶▶ The international language for fencing is French and you may hear some referees using unfamiliar terminology. Fluency is not needed to follow what is going on, but the most common French terms are "en garde," "prêt?," "allez," meaning on guard, ready? fence.

A white light indicates an off target touch while a valid touch produces a colored light, red or green. If you are fencing on a metallic strip, any touches accidentally made on the strip will be grounded out and the scoring lights will not come on. When your bout ends, you shake your opponent's hand with your ungloved, non-fencing hand. By rule you must salute the referee at the end of a bout and should also salute your opponent but usually a handshake suffices. When disconnecting your body cord from the reel, be careful to walk the reel socket back to the reel because letting it go may very well damage the wire when it strikes the reel under the tension of the reel's spring.

Competitive Ratings

When you register with the bout committee at a meet, you will be asked for your rating so that pools can be made up with a balanced distribution of skill levels. Most beginners are unclassified, or U, until such time as they do well in a competition. I won't get into the complex formulas for advancing in rank but the highest classification is A, then B, C, D, and E in descending order. Ratings are based entirely on meet performance and not at all on form or knowledge. If a fencer is rated as C-04, this means the C rating was earned in 2004. A rating is valid for three years and will then drop to the next level unless it is renewed in competition or a higher level is achieved.

> ▶▶▶ There are competitions for various skill levels and for ages ranging from those for Youth 10 years and younger on up to Veterans 60 and older. Wherever you live, you will be a member of a Division that is part of a Section of the United States Fencing Association. The officers of a division are responsible, among other things, for scheduling and conducting local competitions including those that qualify fencers for the national championships.

Penalties

As a competitive fencer, you will need to know the rules and the penalties for violating the rules. There are several common violations that result in receiving a warning card from the referee. For example, a fencer may not turn his back to the opponent, cannot use his unarmed hand to cover target or deflect a blade, and must not cause body contact. Any of these warrant a **yellow penalty card,** which is a warning for the first offense, and **red penalty cards** for additional violations thereafter in that bout. Each red card results in a point for the opponent of the penalized fencer. Figure 17 presents penalties in the first group which are the most commonly found in competition. There are penalties in three other groups with which referees must be familiar; violations in those groups are generally of a more severe type.

The only penalty for stepping off the side of the strip with one or both feet is that the referee stops the bout and has the opponent move forward one meter. If a fencer steps off the strip side with one foot and scores a touch before the bout was halted, the touch will count. A touch made by a fencer who had both feet off the strip cannot be awarded even if a halt had not been called. However, the opponent can score an immediate hit if it is made before the halt. Going off the end of the strip with both feet results not in a penalty card but in a point for the opponent.

Offense	Article	Penalties		
1st Group		**1st**	**2nd**	**3rd and add'l**
Leaving the strip without permission	t.18/3			
Símple Corps à corps (foil and sabre)*	t.20			
Corps à corps to avoid a touch (*)	t.20, t.63			
Turning the back to the opponent (*)	t.21			
Using the non-weapon arm or hand (*)	t.22	Y	R	R
Touching/taking hold of electrical equipment*	t.22	E	E	E
Covering/substitution of valid target*	t.22, t.49, t.72	L	D	D
Crossing the side of the strip to avoid being touched	t.28	L		
Delaying the bout	t.31	O	C	C
Straightening weapon on conductive strip	t.46, t.61, t.70/d	W	A	A
Clothing/equipment not working or not conforming; absence of second regulation weapon or body cord	t.45/1 & 3.b		R	R
Bending/dragging weapon point on conductive strip (F, E)	t.46, t.61	C	D	D
Grounding the weapon on the metallic vest (F) (*)	t.53	A		
In Sabre, touch scored with the guard; (*) any forward movement crossing the legs or feet (*)	t.70, t.75/3	R		
Refusal to obey the referee	t.82, t.84	D		
Jostling, disorderly fencing (*); taking off mask before the referee calls "Halt"; undressing on the strip	t.87			
Unjustified appeal	t.122			
Abnormal fencing action (*)				
Hits with brutality or while falling (*)				

*Annulment of any touch scored by the fencer at fault.
Yellow Card = Warning (valid for bout, whether one or several encounters)
Red Card = Penalty touch

Figure 17. *A Partial U.S.F.A. Penalty Chart*

An Introduction to Épée Fencing

My emphasis so far has been on foil fencing because it is the best weapon for the beginner to learn and is traditionally taught first. However, to be a knowledgeable fencer, you should be at least conversant with the other two weapons regarding target area, rules, and basic techniques. If you are like most fencers, you may be sufficiently curious to want to try the épée or saber, and, who knows, you might find one of these to be more appealing than the foil.

The material covered in this chapter is intended only as an introduction and is not as detailed as what was presented in the previous chapters on foil fencing. I have assumed that the reader is already reasonably competent with the foil and is familiar with terminology and strategies. Realistically, you should seek out an instructor so as to learn correct technique and avoid developing bad habits. Should you not have access to a teacher, this chapter will give you enough of the basics to help you to start learning on your own. Of course you will need a partner with whom to practice, and you will both need to wear full protective gear. Épée is seldom taught in physical education classes because costly full uniforms would have to be provided.

As you will see, everything that you have read about foil fencing earlier in this book has application to the épée. The stance, footwork, and tactics are quite similar and won't be described. The parries and offensive actions learned in foil require some modification when applied to the épée. (Note that the pronunciation is ay-pay due to the French accent marks over the é to give it the ay sound).

While foil and saber fencing can be practiced non-electrically, it is best to use electric épée equipment as soon as you can afford to buy it. However, it is quite all right to

Figure 18. *A Pistol Grip Electric Épée and Body Cord*

start out with "dry" non-electric weapons. As regarding equipment purchase, the major decision is about choosing a grip, and the advice given earlier about foil grips is equally applicable to the épée. For purposes of safety, you and your partner should have full uniforms on when practicing.

Before going into specifics, you need some basic information about the épée. The entire body is valid target, and for that reason the large, off-centered bell is designed to protect the hand. As in foil, only thrusting actions count since both weapons require depression of the push-button tip to activate the scoring light.

There is **no right of way** in this weapon, and whoever hits first gets the point. If both fencers land touches within about one-twentieth of a second of each other, then each will receive a point. Otherwise, the first touch will block out a hit by the other fencer. Because there is no off target, there are no white lights when fencing with the épée, and a lamé is not worn. As is true for the foil and saber, the bell is grounded so that a hit on it will not register on the scoring box.

The strip rules and fencing time are the same as in foil. In competitions, the fencing is done on a grounded metallic strip so that inadvertent touches on the strip, especially missed toe touch attempts, will not be recorded on the scoring box. Where a grounded strip is not available, floor judges must be assigned to specifically watch for hits made on the floor.

Épée is the most spectator-friendly weapon because the rules are simple to understand. With no priority involved, the fencers are not at the mercy of incorrect calls by referees. The concept of "to hit and not be hit" is more prominent in this weapon than in the other two. Épée fencing requires considerable discipline and is the closest we have to real dueling (in fact it had long been called the dueling sword). Without concerns about priority, the referee's task is somewhat easier than it is in foil, because the scoring box pretty much determines the touches to be awarded.

Basic Épée Techniques

As stated earlier, the on guard stance, the footwork, the lunge, and the parries are essentially the same as they are in foil, so you are already well on the way to learning épée. Although competitive fencers hold their weapons in a variety of positions, I like my beginners to be on guard with the blade horizontal and the point directed at the opponent's bell. Because the hand and forearm are prime targets, the fencers normally stand farther apart than they would in foil fencing. Unlike in the foil, it is not common to refer to "lines" since the valid target includes the entire body and there is less use for that terminology. As described for foil, the rear arm can be held in either the classic position or in the modern position.

Figure 19. *Épée On Guard Stance*

In electric épée fencing, when you are called to the strip, the referee will place a 750 gram weight on the tip of your vertically held weapon to see if the spring will raise the weight after the tip is depressed. A second test involves the use of a 0.5 mm gauge placed between the tip and the barrel. The scoring box should not register a touch when the tip is depressed with the gauge in place. Finally, you will touch your tip to your opponent's bell to be sure that his weapon is grounded. As in foil, if your weapon or body cord is defective, you will receive a yellow card. The referee will also look behind your bell to be sure that the wires have proper insulating tubes and will check the tip for missing screws.

> ▶▶▶ Prior to the use of the electric weapon and even to the late 1940s, bouts were fought with épées that had a tip made up of three very sharp, short points protruding about 1/16" from some layers of tape. Between the points, a dab of red gel was placed, and when a touch was scored, the judges would raise their hands and look for a telltale red mark on the jacket. If there was an apparent double touch, the referee had the difficult task of deciding which fencer hit first. After each touch the gel would then be wiped off the jacket with a mild acid solution and the tip re-gelled before the bout could be resumed. You can imagine that bouts lasted some time and jacket sleeves were often torn by the sharp "pointes d'arret." The electric épée was a welcome development.

Defensive Skills

If you are patient and carefully analyze your opponent's manner of attacking, you can make a decision regarding which defensive tactic you will use. The primary defensive choices are the stop hit to the arm and the parry.

Stop hits are very common and effective but require excellent timing and accuracy because, if you miss, you will almost always be hit. The use of a stop hit is an obvious defensive choice when you fence someone who exposes some part of her arm when attacking, especially so if the attack is directed at your foot.

A second choice defensively is to parry attacks made to your body or upper arm, preferably by using the circle parry six. You must be careful to not use the foil riposte that you have spent so much time perfecting because you might be touched by the attacker's remise before your riposte lands. Remember that a parry does not give any priority; it is simply a matter of who touches first so it is important to use some bell opposition when riposting. It is often effective to do the circle six and riposte in a single action, that is, by extending the arm during the parry.

If the parry four is to be used, it should be very short, perhaps in the manner of a beat parry, so that the riposte can be delivered before the attacker's remise hits. Another reason for using a very narrow parry is that it would be more difficult for an opponent to deceive.

A third defense is to retreat out of distance with the weapon arm fully extended to protect it from a touch. Your point will be aimed at the attacker's arm with the hope of getting a "lucky" touch, but your primary concern is protecting yourself. Whether you are attacking, defending, or riposting, keep your hand and arm behind the protection of your bell.

Lastly, if you can maintain good distance at all times, your opponent will not be able to reach your body with a lunge and will be limited to attacking your hand, wrist, or forearm. Such attacks can be defended by using "bell parries," that is, very slight protective movements of your bell while keeping your own point directed at the opponent's arm.

If both you and your opponent have similar guard styles and have arms well-covered by the bells, each will have some difficulty finding an open target to hit. Sooner or later, one of you will make the mistake of coming out from behind the protection offered by the bell and will suffer a stop hit. This style of épée fencing requires patience and self-control.

There are countless invitations that can trick an opponent into attacking you in a way that you are prepared to parry or stop hit. The simplest is to be on guard with your arm purposely but subtly showing. You hope that your opponent will bite and try to touch you and that you will be able to easily parry and score. A more complex invitation is to make a blade movement toward your opponent's blade to try to get her to deceive and attack you when you are ready to parry and riposte. Another tactic is to stand on guard with your arm fully extended as a way of daring your opponent to try to beat or bind. Of course you had better have a plan to deal with those attempts, such as by deceiving or parrying the attacks.

All of the foregoing skills and tactics are elementary, but they form the basis of a sound defense. With more experience, you will find considerable use for the parries two, seven, and eight against attacks under your hand or to some lower body part. For now, it is important to be patient, keep correct distance, and keep your hand and arm covered at all times.

Offensive Skills

Offensive actions are similar to those in foil but very often are directed to the opponent's forearm rather than to the body. This is an adjustment that has to be made by a foilist who is accustomed to attacking only the torso. Also, the foilist has to remember that there is no priority rule and must learn to be wary of stop hits to his arm while on the attack. It is absolutely essential to keep your arm behind your bell whenever you lunge as well as during recovery.

Épée fencers generally avoid using many compound attacks because of the ever-present risk of stop hits. As in foil fencing, feints must be convincing if deceptions are to follow. When your attack fails to score it could be because you simply missed or your opponent parried. If you miss, try a quick redoublement at the end of your lunge and immediately begin recovering. If your attack was parried, you should recover either with an extended arm or with a parry, preferably six. However, if your opponent typically does not riposte, you can remain in the lunge and redouble while being sure that your own arm is not exposed. Remises and redoublements are much more common in épée than they are in foil.

Three lunge distances can be defined. A short lunge is made to the opponent's hand or wrist. Medium-length lunges will reach the upper arm, and long lunges are made to the body or toe. Be advised however that until you are ready to attack, you should maintain a long distance that would require your opponent to make a full lunge just to reach your hand.

Toe touches can be effective against converted foil fencers who are accustomed to defending only the torso. But, needless to say, any attacks directed to the toe will necessarily expose your arm to stop hits, so know beforehand what to expect from your opponent. You might try a false lunge toward the hand to draw a parry which you would avoid and then complete the lunge to the toe. Even if your toe attempt fails, it can cause some anxiety in your opponent regarding how to defend if you threaten her toe again. Not many fencers find success with attacks to the toe, and a beginner should not even try.

False lunges are important to detect your opponent's defensive plans and to mask the start of your real attacks. Second intention actions are just as important in épée as they are in foil. For example, you could fake a toe touch, parry your

Figure 20. *A Toe Touch*

opponent's stop hit, and score with your riposte. Or you could use a false lunge to draw a parry four, parry the anticipated riposte, and then bind with your own riposte.

If you encounter an opponent whose style is to fence with a fully extended arm, you can utilize beats or any of the prises de fer such as a bind to control your opponent's blade as you attack. But it is likely that straight-arm fencers have experience in dealing with those who attempt to beat or bind and are adept at deceiving. Your solution might be to make a fake binding movement, allow the deception, and then make the real bind, which is less likely to be deceived. Also remember that you can make beats in a direction other than the one which the defender is expecting. Every problem has a solution.

While it is not an essential skill, the flèche may be necessitated by your inability to otherwise reach your opponent, but do not use it unless you have trained yourself to do it properly. As I mentioned in chapter 7, this can be a dangerous attack if made with a stiff arm that might cause the blade to break and injure the opponent. Tall fencers seldom have to use it, but for the shorter fencer it provides an alternative means of delivering the blade to a distant target.

There is an element of luck in épée fencing as when an opponent impales his arm on your point much to your surprise. But a touch is a touch, and you must have done something right if your point was there to be run onto. Strategies are not much different than in foil fencing, and I dare say that a competent foil fencer could do a decent job of fencing épée without formal instruction. The reverse is not quite as easy because of priority rules and the smaller foil target.

In a competition, double touches can be a major factor in épée fencing. For example, if you are leading 4–2, you can afford to attack or counter-attack in some manner that risks a double touch that would win the bout for you. Even if you failed, the score would still be 4–3 in your favor. By the same token, if you are trailing by that score, you have to score clean hits and avoid double touches. It may happen that you were hit but thought that you had also hit. In such cases be sure to have the referee test your weapon because if it fails, the opponent's touch would be annulled. Never test the weapon yourself first; let the referee do it.

Safety is a major concern in this weapon because the blade is quite stiff and won't bend much on a hard touch, as would a more flexible foil blade. It is advisable for a male épéeist to wear a groin cup. At least in practice bouts, you should never purposely aim for the mask even though it is part of the target. The jolt is uncomfortable and there is the very slight chance that the mask could be severely dented into the face or, very rarely, penetrated.

Drills

▶   I think that "shadow fencing" in front of a full-length mirror is very useful. The mirror shows you what your opponent sees, especially any part of your forearm that may be exposed as you simulate attacks and parries.

▶   A common device to improve accuracy is a ball suspended by a long cord from the ceiling. An old tennis ball with an eyehook screwed into it serves this purpose very well, but some prefer a smaller ball. The pendular motion makes the ball hard to hit, and if you lunge and miss, you should redouble once before recovering. As the ball swings, keep your point aimed at it.

▶   With a cooperating partner, a "defender" will expose some part of her arm and the "attacker" will lunge to hit it. If the defender moves the arm a bit to cause the attacker to miss, the attacker must immediately redouble once or twice, being sure to keep her own arm covered. The defender might occasionally use a surprise parry and riposte to keep the attacker alert.

If you refer to the foil drills in appendix C, you will find many ideas which, with minor changes, apply as well to the épée as to the foil. Emphasis should be on doing drills that end in a touch to the arm.

In conclusion, épée fencing is the least complex of the three weapons, but its very simplicity makes it quite difficult. There is a lot of target to defend, and accuracy on the attack and riposte is crucial. More so than in foil or saber, tall fencers have some advantage in this weapon.

> ▶▶▶ **Five touches are needed to win a bout in all three weapons. An exception is the épée event in the Modern Pentathlon in which only a single touch is required to win. The other four events are shooting, riding, swimming, and running. For many years participation in the Modern Pentathlon was limited to military officers for whom the events held special significance. Such is no longer the case since the use of cavalry and swords in war is obsolete.**

Self-Testing Questions

1. Describe ways in which foil and épée are similar.

2. Why is attempting a lunge to the toe risky?

3. Which parry is the most commonly used?

4. Does a point in line give an épée fencer priority?

5. Why doesn't an épée fencer need to wear a lamé?

6. What happens when there are simultaneous touches?

An Introduction to Saber Fencing

As I stated at the start of the last chapter on épée, it is important for students of fencing to have an overall knowledge of the sport even if they expect to fence only with the foil. The saber holds appeal for individuals who are quick and aggressive and like to fight. The slashing movements in saber fencing resemble the kind of swordplay one often sees in swashbuckling movies, whereas foils are seldom used in films. Thus the public's impressions regarding fencing pretty much center on cutting styles more so than thrusting. Perhaps beginning students who have seen Zorro, for example, might expect instruction in saber and could possibly be turned off when handed a foil. This is supposition on my part, as I have never actually encountered resistance in my classes to learning foil rather than saber.

There is no reason why a beginner should not be taught to fence with the saber without first learning foil. But I would recommend that this be done in private lessons rather than in a physical education class. For one thing, saber requires more equipment—full jackets, gloves, and three-weapon masks—which would make it more costly. Once you have learned foil fencing reasonably well, you will find that much of your training and knowledge will readily transfer to saber fencing. Priority, stance, footwork, lunging, defending, and strategies are common to both weapons.

> ▶ ▶ ▶ Until relatively recently, the rather conservative F.I.E. limited women to competing only with the foil, but now they can fence competitively with any of the three weapons. It was not until 2004 that women's saber was added as an Olympic event (women's épée had been added in 1996 and women's foil in 1924).

The bells and blades of all three weapons have different shapes. The saber handle is the same for both left and right handers, but the bell guard for a right handed fencer is wider on the right side to afford better protection to the forearm. Saber blades bend left or right rather than up and down as in foil.

The main similarity between saber and foil is the rule of right of way. As in foil, the attacker has priority and a successful parry gives a defender the right to riposte. The **target** in saber includes the mask and all parts of the body above a horizontal line drawn between the top of the creases formed between the thighs and the abdomen. The hands are not part of the target. Not too long ago, the fencing hand was a valid part of the target and the glove was covered with metallic material, but referees often had difficulty distinguishing between a successful parry and a parry over which the flexible blade whipped around the bell guard and struck the hand. A new regulation was passed to require stiffer blades to help reduce the number of such whipover touches.

While the saber's point may be used, nearly all touches are scored with cutting actions using any part of the blade. In electric saber, a fencer wears a lamé that covers the target area including the arms up to the wrist joints. Since the mask is also valid target, it has to be completely conductive and is connected to the fencer's metallic vest by means of a short cable. The body cord is the same as that used in foil and can be either a bayonet or two-prong type.

Electric saber equipment is more costly than the other weapons but at least the saber itself, having no moving parts, requires no maintenance outside of replacing broken blades. There is no tip to depress and blade contact with the lamé completes the circuit. As with the other two weapons, the saber bell is grounded, and hits on the bell will not register on the scoring box.

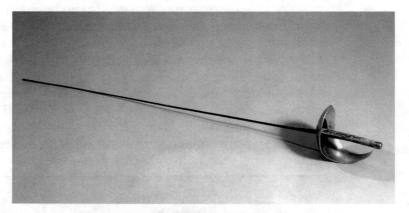

Figure 21. *A Saber*

Basic Saber Techniques

The on guard stance is similar to that used in the other weapons with the exception that the rear arm is not held up in the classic position of a foil fencer. There is usually a fairly large angle formed between the saber blade and the fencing forearm, and the fencing hand is slightly pronated in the third position. The distance between two fencers is considerably greater than it is in foil.

Instead of describing lines, saber target areas can be referred to as the head, the cheek, the chest, the arm, and the flank, which is the fencing arm side of the body. Any of these targets may be attacked offensively or counter-offensively with ripostes. Stop cuts to an opponent's forearm are commonly used during the attacker's preparation. Such cuts should be made with the very end of the saber blade and accompanied by a retreat and a parry as protection should the stop cut fail. Remember that attacks have priority over stop cuts, so you must hit *before* the final phase of the opponent's compound action.

Figure 22. *Saber On Guard Stance (the gray lamé covers the valid target)*

Defensive Skills

Against attacks made to the flank or the outside of the weapon arm, saber fencers use the parry three because the weapon hand is already in the pronated third position when on guard. The parry four is similar to the foil parry but there is some rotation of the hand so that the blade's cutting edge meets the incoming cut to the chest. Ripostes are always by cut rather than thrust and may be directed to any open target, either directly or indirectly after a feint. Generally, parries are made wider than they would be in foil fencing.

Against vertical cuts to your head, you could defend with lateral parries three or four, but the parry that is specific to this attack is the **parry five.** In the classic parry five shown in figure 23, the blade would be at head level, with the point higher than the hand and slightly forward. The riposte could be directly to the opponent's flank or by a circular cut to the head or chest.

If an opponent's feint effectively causes you to assume this parry position, your chest and flank are wide open to a cut. To avoid being quite so open against a feint-cut attack, a defender can use a compromise version of the parry five wherein the saber hand moves to a position somewhere between five and three, that is, higher than a parry three but lower than a parry five.

You may find occasional use for the parry two, which is similar to the foil parry. If a feint to your head causes you to start to parry five and you realize that the real attack is being directed to your flank, you have two defensive choices.

Figure 23. *Saber Parry Five*

You could bring your hand back down to the third parry, or you could lower your hand and blade to a parry two.

As an alternative to parry four, you can use a parry one, which is essentially identical to the foil parry one shown in figure 13a, and make your riposte by circular cut to the head or chest. This parry is somewhat obsolete, but because it is so uncommon, it may cause some confusion for the opponent.

The defense most relied upon is the quick retreat. Parrying is extremely difficult because there is so much target to defend and attacks can come from so many directions. A typical defensive tactic is to retreat as rapidly as the opponent is advancing while making a varying pattern of blade movements in quick succession, including point in line, to occupy the attacker's attention and to obscure any openings. All through his retreats the defender is watching for opportunities to **stop cut** to the arm or to attack into the opponent's preparatory advances. If the attack is concluded and fails, the defender will often take over and become the aggressively closing attacker.

As in foil, a point in line has priority, and you as a defender may utilize it to temporarily hold off an aggressive opponent. It can be easily beaten, however, so do not maintain a point in line when your opponent moves close enough to make a beat.

All ripostes must be made very quickly because the current "blocking" times in the scoring boxes favor an attacker's remise if there is any delay in the riposte. In summary of the options available to you when defending, you can parry, retreat, and attack or stop cut into preparation. But you really need an offensive ability to succeed as a saber fencer.

Offensive Skills

The saber is the only weapon in which the flèche is prohibited by rule. In the past, fencers had been overusing it to the point where every phrase seemed to involve two fencers just running at one another. What had once been an interesting and exciting event deteriorated so much that spectators did not enjoy watching it, and referees were hard-pressed to establish priority for either fencer. The penalty for crossing the rear foot ahead of the front foot is now a yellow card and annulment of a touch that was made by the violator.

Even today, sabermen often do simultaneous advance lunges repeatedly at each command to "fence," partly because it is so difficult to defend the large target area that parries cannot be depended upon. Both fencers typically advance lunge with perhaps one feint and a cut. The result is "no touch" since both appear to have had equal priority. This pattern may be repeated two or three times, each time resulting in no points unless one fencer happens to hit the bell of the other and is thereby parried. The referee's task in determining priority is extremely difficult because of the numerous simultaneous attacks.

A major problem for a referee is in distinguishing between a beat by one fencer and a parry by the other. This requires the referee to judge intent, which might be based on his observation of the particular fencers' actions in previous phrases. A beat made on an opponent's blade close to the bell, the forte, is interpreted by the referee as being a parry.

There are usually more touches made by well-timed direct cuts than by feint and cut. But if you are just learning this weapon, you need to practice making the feint of a cut to some target, deceiving the likely parry, and hitting the target opened by the feint. Such deceptions are normally done in the manner of a foil cutover rather than by passing under the parry attempt, but be very careful to not lift your hand because of the risk of a stopcut.

> ▶▶▶ **Before the electric saber came into use, cuts with the saber had to be made with either the front cutting-edge of the blade or with the forward one third of the back edge in a draw cut manner. Flat hits were not called by the judges and were considered to have missed.**

Of course, you can use your point as you do in foil by straight thrust, feint and disengage, one-two, or double. But these are not common in saber and your effort should be directed to learning to use the blade edge. If you do use your point, lunge with your hand palm down in pronation because disengagements are more easily made from that position.

In a situation where a non-electric saber competition is held, the judging positions, procedures, and voting are identical to those described in appendix D for non-electric foil bouts. The judges will often not see quick, light touches, and there is a tendency for the fencers to hit a bit harder so that their touches are both visible and audible. Welts are common.

Finally, as mentioned earlier, crossing the rear leg ahead of the front leg is a flèche and will result in a yellow card, so innovative saber fencers have been using a "**flunge**" which is a sort of combination of lunge and flèche. The fencer makes a long lunge and then, without interruption, hops forward onto the leading foot so that the rear leg never crosses over illegally. It certainly covers a long distance, but it is a difficult skill for a beginner who should stick with the more controllable lunges and advance lunges.

Drills

▶   Learn to hit lightly for greatest efficiency. With a cooperating, stationary partner, make several lunges to each of the primary targets—the head, the chest, and the flank. Cut from the wrist rather than from the elbow.

▶ As with the above drill, your partner will attack each of your targets and you will do the appropriate parry for each, including the circle parry three. Hold the parry without riposting to check on correctness.

▶ Now add the riposte after your parry. From each parry, practice direct ripostes to the partner's head, flank, or chest while the partner remains in the lunge and allows the hit.

▶ Practice feinting a cut to either of the target areas and deceiving the partner's pre-arranged parry while also lunging to hit quickly and lightly.

▶ Do the above with an advance lunge.

▶ The partner will raise his weapon hand during an advance lunge and the defender will stop cut to the exposed forearm and immediately step back out of distance while also parrying in case the stop cut fails.

▶ Do the leader-follower drill that you learned earlier for foil. Emphasize short, rapid footwork.

▶ To further motivate you to increase your footwork speed, try the steps per second drill that is described in appendix C. The ability to do fast retreats is essential in saber and should be done while slightly inclining the body forward. By doing so, if you decide to make a sudden stop, you will be less likely to lose balance.

This is now a sport for quick athletes. There are very few prolonged phrases wherein there is an attack, a parry-riposte, and a parry-counter riposte. Tactics mostly revolve around rapid movement, opportunism, and decisive action.

> ▶▶▶ Saber was the last weapon to be electrified because there was no agreement about how best to deal with touches made below the lamé. In 1976 the F.I.E. insisted that whatever scoring system was developed had to be able to record off-target hits. In non-electric saber such low hits stopped the bout since they were "off-target." Finally, it was decided to eliminate the off-target touch rule; thus there is no white light for an invalid touch as there is in foil. A low hit is now just a miss and is not recorded on the scoring box. In the 2004 Olympics, saber was fenced with wireless equipment without reels. It is unlikely that this equipment will be affordable for most clubs and will not be mandated for saber meets in the foreseeable future.

Women's Electric Saber

Self-Testing Questions

1. Why is there no white light when the scoring box is on the saber setting?

2. How does a saber mask differ from masks used in the other two weapons?

3. What rule is shared with foil fencing?

4. Which body parts are not considered to be valid target?

5. Which form of attack that is permitted in the other two weapons is not legal in saber?

6. Which parry is specifically used to defend against attacks to the head?

Appendix A

Equipment Selection

For those of you who are enrolled in a college fencing course or in any other class where the necessary equipment is provided, the information in this appendix can be skipped for now. If you later become serious about the sport, then of course you will need to purchase your own equipment and might find some helpful suggestions here.

As is true in most sports, fencing equipment comes in a range of prices directly related to quality. For the best fit, durability, and safety, get the highest quality equipment that you can afford, especially if you know that you will be fencing for a long time. Everything that you will need can be purchased online. Most vendors have web sites showing their stock and prices (find the links on www.usfencing.org). If you are strictly a recreational fencer, you can save a bit of money by ordering a starter set which usually includes a French foil, mask, gloves, and jacket.

Ordering can be perplexing for new fencers. There are so many types of foil grips from which to choose, and it is difficult to know what jacket and mask sizes to request and from which company to buy. Your instructor, and especially your club-mates, can be very helpful in your decisions. If you are on your own, I suggest that you purchase equipment and uniforms by telephone in order to get advice on sizing and to ask questions. If you are left-handed, be sure to mention that when ordering foils, gloves, or jackets.

Foils

There are two basic types of foil grips—the French and the pistol. As a beginner you will not know which type of handle will be best for you, and at first you will probably use whatever your instructor provides. But if the choice is yours, try the grips of other fencers to find which will fit your hand best since there are many variations of pistol grip designs and sizes. My own preference for beginners is the French grip, especially for class use, because it is less expensive, one size fits all, and maintenance is easier. That grip also allows for better use of the fingers in learning to manipulate the foil. French foil handles may be made of wood, metal, or plastic and may be covered with rubber, cord, or leather. Pistol grips are usually made of aluminum or plastic.

Blades are generally 35 inches in length, never longer, but also come in 30, 32, and 34 inches, typically designated as 0, 2, or 4, with the shorter being best suited to young children. The length and threads of blade tangs (the part that passes through the handle) are different for French and pistol foils and may have either metric 6 mm or U.S. 12–24 threads. It is important to give the vendor the correct information when buying replacement blades to ensure compatibility with your foil's pommel and grip.

Finally, some foils have blades that are very stiff while others are quite "soft," that is to say flexible, and you should indicate your preference when ordering. You will need to work a slight downward bend into the end one-fourth of a new blade by sliding it back and forth between your shoe and the floor until you get a bit of a curve. This curve will allow the blade to bend when a touch is scored and thus reduce the slight shock of impact. Be sure to cover the tip of a non-electric foil with either a plastic or rubber tip, available commercially, or with several layers of adhesive tape.

Figure 24. *A Disassembled French Foil (L to R beneath the blade: bell, thumb pad, handle, pommel)*

On a French foil the pommel serves two purposes, one being that its weight helps to counterbalance the blade's weight to make it easier to hold the foil, and secondly that it holds the foil parts together. To replace a broken blade, the pommel can be unscrewed to free the various parts and allow a new blade with a similar tang and threading to be inserted. For pistol foils, the pommel is small and serves only to hold the parts together without having any balance benefit. Some pistol grip pommels can be unscrewed with a screwdriver while others require either a commonly available inside hex wrench or an outside hex wrench that can be purchased from a fencing equipment vendor.

Uniforms

Uniforms are available in a wide range of materials and protective qualities from which to choose. Jackets and trousers may be made of stretch fabrics or of somewhat more robust canvas. Proper fit is of course important to allow freedom of movement. Many serious competitors wear only uniforms designated with the F.I.E. label (Federation Internationale d'Escrime, the international governing body); these are more costly but are required for competing in international meets and provide the highest puncture resistance. For the casual fencer, almost any jacket available through vendors is safe enough for practice.

Jacket sizes may be given as small through extra large, may be numerical by chest measurement, or may even have a European size. As mentioned earlier, ordering a jacket by phone is more likely to result in a correct fit because you can describe your height and build and let the vendor judge the correct size to ship. Some starter jackets are back zipped, are cheaper, and can be used by either right or left-handed fencers, all of which are advantages if the jackets are to be used in class situations. They can be a nuisance to zip up, so you might consider paying a bit more for a front closing design.

Knickers are ordered by waist measurements and some companies offer longer lengths for tall fencers. They are required for competition, as are knee length stockings, an underarm protective garment, and a breast protector for women. There are shoes designed specifically for fencing, but for the novice, any low cut, preferably white, court shoe will serve quite well. I would not recommend wearing cleated running shoes.

Masks

As with uniforms, you get what you pay for when ordering a mask. Again, the least expensive mask will likely be adequate for the recreational fencer, but the advanced competitor needs a mask which will do more than just barely pass the 12 kg punch test at a meet. That test is done with a small hand-held instrument which, when pressed against the mesh of the mask, should not penetrate the mesh.

Masks usually come in small, medium, and large sizes, and the fit is correct if the mask is comfortable and fits firmly enough on the head that it will not come off during a bout. Fencers who wear glasses may have to try various models to determine which will not press against the frames. The major problem with modern masks is that they are hot, and the inside padding and sewn-in bibs are difficult to keep clean after perspiration has soaked in. As a partial solution, some companies offer masks that have removable, washable bib liners.

For international saber competitions, masks with transparent visors are now required. Such masks may in the near future be required for the other weapons as well. This should not be a concern for recreational fencers or those involved with beginning classes.

Gloves

One of the least expensive items on your list of needs is a fencing glove. The sizes may be small, medium, large, or extra large, or may come in numerical sizes. Gloves are lightly padded and have long cuffs to cover the wrist and part of the forearm to prevent an opponent's blade from going up the inside of the sleeve. Most gloves have an opening near the wrist to permit the passage of an electric body cord. A fencer who is prone to perspiring heavily might consider purchasing a washable glove.

Other Items

The rules require that a competitive fencer wear an underarm garment under the jacket to provide an extra layer of protection to the chest as well as the armpit area of the foil arm. These are inexpensive and can be ordered in small, medium, and large sizes.

Women who compete must wear any one of several types of breast protection, and while not required, many men also choose to wear plastic chest guards to reduce the discomfort of hard hits by electric foils or épées. It is prudent for men to have some sort of groin protection for reasons that should be obvious.

Appendix B

Selection, Maintenance, and Repair of Electric Equipment

Competitive fencers must own the basic equipment needed for electric fencing. In all three weapons a body cord is necessary to form part of the connection between the fencer and the scoring apparatus. For foil and saber, a metallic vest called a lamé or conductive jacket exactly covers the valid target area and is worn over the regular fencing jacket. A special, completely conductive mask is required for use in electric saber. An épée fencer does not need a lamé because the entire body is valid target.

For competitions, the rules stipulate that a fencer must come to the strip with at least two weapons and a spare body cord, because should a weapon or body cord fail or break during a bout, a quick replacement can be made without unduly delaying the meet. At major competitions, a foil fencer must have his or her last name stenciled onto the rear trouser leg or onto the back of the lamé, or in épée on the back of the jacket. This obviously aids others to identify the fencer from a distance.

Selecting Equipment

If you are new to the sport, it would be prudent to seek purchasing advice from some advanced club-mates especially regarding your choice of a foil grip. I can tell you that most fencers use one of the several shapes and sizes of pistol grips, but if you are comfortable with the French handle there is no reason not to stay with it. I cannot advise you as to which pistol grip style would be best for your hand and can only urge that you try as many types as you can at your club. Some grips come in only one size while others can be purchased in sizes ranging from small to large.

The next concern is which of the two common kinds of connecting socket you want on your foil or saber. You can't go wrong with either a two-prong or a bayonet socket, but whichever you select, be sure that the body cords you purchase will fit your socket. If you are going to compete, you will need a minimum of two electric weapons and two body cords, so get them all from the same vendor to be sure that the grips are identical and the parts are compatible. While ordering, find out what type of pommel will be on your foils because you may need to order a special tool to have on hand to keep the pommel tight or to use for some future repairs.

As with non-electric blades, you can request blade lengths between 30 inches, suitable for young children, and the more common maximum 35 inches. If you are likely to flick a lot, you will want a somewhat whippy blade, and if you often break blades, you might consider spending more money to buy a *maraging* blade which is made of specially treated materials and may last a long time. To order a replacement for a broken blade, you need to know whether its tang has a metric 6 mm or a U.S. 12-24 threading so that you can be sure that your pommel will fit. Replacement blades for a French grip will usually fit easily, but since there are so many shapes and sizes of pistol grips, you may have to use a hack saw to cut a blade's tang to fit your grip.

There are two types of foil tips in common use, the French and the German, and the replacement screws and springs are not interchangeable. Each kind has its advocates, but beginners will likely use whatever types are sent by the vendor.

After you have chosen an electric foil, you will also need a metallic vest, called a lamé, to wear over your regular jacket. The lamé acts as one of the links in completing the electric circuit when a valid touch is made. Lamés come in jacket sizes and are cut to cover only your target area. Some have a zipper in the back and have the advantage of being a bit cheaper and can be worn by either right or left-handed fencers. I suggest that you pay a bit more and get a lamé that closes in the front, either with a zipper or Velcro. If cared for, a lamé will last several years.

Maintenance and Repair

Even with regular basic maintenance of electric foils and body cords, there will come a time when they fail. Some problems are relatively easy to fix, but if your foil needs rewiring you would do well to seek advice from someone who has had some experience with repairs. The following information admittedly is not comprehensive but should suffice to deal with the more common problems of your foil or body cord.

Electric foil uses a fail-safe system, meaning that current flows continuously and is interrupted by depressing the foil tip or by a break in the foil wire, body cord, floor cable, or reel. A defect *anywhere* in the circuit will cause a white light on the scoring box. You are responsible only for your foil and body cord, so if there is a problem, start with the simple checks. If you and a partner are hooked up for fencing, try switching foils with one another to see if a white light still shows. If it doesn't, the fault is probably in your body cord.

The fault may show up only intermittently, so try shaking the body cord at each end to see if a white light comes on. If the barrel at the tip end seems to be loose, tighten it with a wrench or a pair of pliers applied to the base of the barrel so as not to distort the tip end. If you still get white lights, examine the foil wire where it connects to the body cord socket to see if it is broken or has come off. Check the tip for a missing or loose screw. Be sure that the pommel is tight because if the bell moves around it might be the source of the problem, and a loose bell might sever the wire where it passes through the bell.

When none of the above attempts to locate the problem is successful, or if you get no light at all when the tip is depressed, the bad news is that the wire is broken or shorted somewhere along the blade or in the tip and your blade will likely require rewiring. You could go the easy but more expensive route and just buy an already wired replacement blade, in which case you can skip the instructions below down to where I describe assembling the foil. But if you want to tackle the job yourself and have a replacement wire and some basic tools listed below, then by all means give it a try. If you have a club mate who has had some experience with rewiring, by all means ask for some guidance.

Step one is disassembling the foil by removing the pommel and carefully noting how all the parts fit so as to be sure to put everything back together correctly. French foil pommels are easy to take off, but there are at least three types of pistol grip pommels, each requiring a different tool for removal. One kind has a slot for a standard screwdriver, and the other two types require either an outside socket wrench or a 6 mm hex key wrench.

The next step is removal of the tape at the end of the blade and unscrewing the two tiny tip screws. Keep a finger on the tip as you take out the screws, otherwise the spring, which is under tension, could send the tip and spring flying. It's a good idea to do all of this over a white cloth or towel because screws have a nasty habit of falling to the floor and bouncing out of sight. Now put the blade in a vise and remove the old wire.

If you are lucky, the glue holding the wire in the groove is a type that will allow you to simply pull the wire out, but some glues hold so fast that the wire will break as you try to remove it. You may be able to soften the glue with some solvent (be sure to do so only in a ventilated area), or you may have to resort to scraping out the wire bit by bit with the back edge of an old knife blade or similar implement. This is the least pleasant task in all of fencing. Be sure that the blade's groove has been thoroughly cleaned of glue and wire remnants before you put in the new wire. Otherwise the replacement wire will not fit properly into the groove.

The next step is to unscrew the barrel and push out the old wire cup that may still be inside. Before proceeding further, check to see if the cup of your new wire will slide easily into the barrel. If it does not, you will have to order a wire that is compatible with your barrel. You can purchase a package containing a wire, barrel, spring, and screws.

Now you reverse the whole process. Insert the new wire into the barrel but don't push the cup in yet. With the blade held in a vise, screw the barrel onto the blade being sure that the wire is loosely resting in the groove and is free to move. Next, pull gently on the wire to seat the cup inside the barrel because a hard tug could break the fragile wire. Working a few inches at a time, apply the glue to the groove and continually press the wire deep into the groove while keeping a light tension on the wire. I use my thumb nail or the back edge of a knife to be sure the wire is well down into the groove, but you must be careful not to damage the wire's insulation.

Set the blade aside for a while until the glue has dried. Then apply a second coat to help prevent the wire from popping out during fencing. If you chose to buy a wired blade instead of going through the above procedures, then what follows is your starting point. Save the tip parts from a broken blade for use in future repairs, but keep them separate from new parts. Film canisters are good for parts storage.

The next step is assembling the foil. Begin by sliding the insulating tubing onto the free end of the wire, leaving about an inch of wire exposed. That bit of wire must be free of insulation before it is attached to the socket. Then put the guard and socket over the blade's tang being sure to pass the wire *through both* the bell and the socket bracket. Attach the uninsulated end of the wire onto the socket, and then put on the thumb pad and the handle and tighten the pommel. Most handles come with a notch cut that helps to prevent crushing the wire against the bracket or bell; be sure that your wires lay inside that notch before you tighten the pommel.

Insert the spring and tip and put in the two tiny screws, which is often an exasperating task with some tip styles because you must line up the hole in the barrel with the hole in the tip's collar. The last step is to tape the end six or seven inches of the blade up to the base of the barrel. Wrap a separate piece of tape once around the barrel to make it easier to peel off if you need to service the tip later. Any electrical tape of any color will serve the purpose.

If all went well, you will have spent an hour on the rewiring task (longer if the old wire was hard to remove), and the weapon will test satisfactorily on your meter or on a scoring box. To test with a volt-ohm meter, set the meter for low ohms (an ohm is a unit of electrical resistance). Touch or attach one of the two leads to the bell or blade and the other to the socket where you attached the wire. If the circuit is complete, the meter's reading will be 1 to 2 ohms, and when you depress the tip, the meter should show an open circuit. Commercial test boxes are available and you may find them to be easier to use than meters, but they may not detect some faults.

As for a bad body cord, the most common problems are a loose wire within one of the two plugs or a break in one of the two wires, typically within a few inches of the foil plug end. Compared with a blade-rewiring job, the repair is usually easy. Test the continuity of the two wires by attaching your meter's leads to the matching plugs at each end of the body cord. If the wire is unbroken, the meter should read less than 2 ohms. Some breaks still make intermittent contact so flex the cord at different spots along the wire to see if and where the meter needle is affected. Frequently, the problem is inside one of the plugs, and in opening the plug case, you can see where a wire may have come loose or been broken. But if you find the break to be in a wire at one of the two ends, cut the wires at the suspected point, disassemble the plug, strip off a bit of the insulation, and reattach the wires to the matching plugs.

Many of the same procedures are used in repairing épées. The épée circuit, however, is the closed type and if your blade or body cord is defective, you will not get a white light on the scoring box to alert you that there is a problem.

> ▶ ▶ ▶ Some clubs are fortunate to have a member who serves as the armorer and has the knowledge and tools needed to maintain the club's scoring box, reels, and weapons. If you have such a person, treat him or her with the utmost respect and even adulation.

A little maintenance before a competition will save you a lot of grief. Be sure that foil tip screws and the pommel are tight. Retape the end of your foil if the old tape is getting frayed. Borrow a weight to check that your foil spring will pass the test. Look carefully down the length of the blade and flex the blade in the direction of the groove to detect a loose wire that needs an application of glue to prevent it from popping out.

To do your own repairs, here is a list of the tools you will need.

▶ A few spare foil wires and tips that are compatible with your foil tip barrel.

▶ A set of jeweler's screwdrivers.

▶ A volt-ohm meter to test for circuit continuity or a test box available through vendors.

▶ A pommel-loosening/tightening tool designed for your pistol grip pommel type.

▶ Any type of fast drying pliable glue (not super glue).

▶ Pliers or a small wrench to use on the foil barrel.

▶ Tape to cover the barrel and several inches of the end of the blade.

▶ Optionally, a glue solvent such as acetone to help in removal of old wire.

▶ A bench vise to hold your blade while you work.

▶ Anticipating problems, keep on hand spare springs, screws, and insulating tubing.

▶ A hack saw.

▶ A soldering iron and resin-core solder.

▶▶▶ Back in the 1930s a famous coach with an engineering background, Bela de Tuscan, invented and patented, in 1942, a tubular foil blade along with an electrical scoring system. The blade was somewhat flat and hollow, which allowed the wire to be *inside* the blade where it could not break or pop out. There were no reels or scoring box because each fencer had a small light mounted on the mask to indicate a touch on the opponent's lamé. The blade was very light and flexible and had a non-moving tip. The scoring system was rejected by the F.I.E. because it could not identify off target touches, and perhaps the tubular blade was just too radical for the traditionalists. In the 2004 Olympics, the saber fencers had lights mounted on their masks, so perhaps de Tuscan was ahead of his time.

But then, consider that in 1896 there was a demonstration of an electric foil. When a touch was made, the blade pressed into the handle to complete a connection through a body cord to a bell in a wall-mounted apparatus. See p. 537 in Thimm's *A Complete Bibliography of Fencing & Dueling*.

Appendix C

Drills

What are your goals as a fencer? Perhaps you are satisfied with your skill level and now want to fence once or twice a week only for fun and exercise. If so, then you may not be interested in doing drills. But if you aspire to compete, and especially if you don't have an instructor to guide you, then some portion of your time at a club should be devoted to drills. You will of course need an equally motivated partner or group to work with because there is only so much that you can do alone.

If you are taking a physical education class, you will undoubtedly be doing a number of drills during the course, some like the ones that follow and some of your instructor's creation. They are an essential part of the learning process.

Even when certain drills might appear to not have practical bout use, they can still be enjoyable, interesting, and challenging if you have the proper mindset, and they can improve self-discipline, coordination, and blade control. Drills offer the chance to hone skills that may be needed in a bout or they can help develop what generations of masters have referred to as **sentiment-de-fer,** a French phrase that implies a sense of feeling through and oneness with the blade. Consider your foil to be an extension of your hand, a long finger as it were.

Once advanced fencers have done a particular drill well enough, one of the partners can occasionally do something unexpected in order to keep the other alert. But the obvious purpose of drills is to achieve a level of perfection under controlled, predictable conditions, and this requires cooperative, motivated partners. Unfortunately, at many clubs everyone just wants to fence and will do drills only when required by the instructor. Drills don't have to last long, but when you recognize some weakness in your skills, you need to take the time to make needed improvements.

Some of the following foil drill suggestions were presented in earlier chapters, but there are many that were not. They are arranged from the simpler to the more complex within the stated headings. All drills can be adapted to suit the needs of a group and can be used to teach a new skill or to improve technique, tactics, concentration, or timing. For convenience, one partner in some drills may be labeled A (attacker) and the other D (defender). Those drills that are not foil-specific can be utilized for the other two weapons with minor modifications.

Footwork Improvement

1. The easiest drill is leader-follower footwork and is suitable for just two students or for any sized class. It is the follower's responsibility to try to stay at lunge distance at all times as the leader advances or retreats in any random pattern. As with all drills, each person should serve the role of teacher in watching for form errors. Even advanced fencers can profit from this exercise if the leader tries hard to "lose" the partner who has to maintain correct distance. If not overdone, these sudden and rapid changes of direction can also serve to improve the condition of the legs. Foils are not needed for this drill, but if they are used, then masks must be worn.

   A variation can be done without foils. The paired partners are on guard with each lightly holding the end of a thin rope of three to four feet in length. The follower must not allow the rope to become limp nor to be jerked from his grasp.

2. A group of three can make the above drill into a point-scoring game. Two will pair off with A being given the role of leader. The third person will time the "bout" for, say, twenty seconds during which he will call out "point" every time that the follower D gets too close or too far from A who of course is attempting to "lose" D in order to gain points. The fencers then rotate until each has "fenced" twice and the scores are compared to see who won. This drill can be done without foils.

3. Partner A will retreat any number of times while D follows. When A comes to a sudden stop, D must instantly stop and begin to retreat as the new leader, and so on. As a variation, D will lead by retreating and whenever D comes to an abrupt stop, A must try to score with a lunge after which the roles change. D should not parry. The first part of this drill can be done without foils, but the second one requires foils, masks, and jackets.

4. As a test of retreating footwork speed, I have used a steps per second test. Draw two lines perhaps five or six feet apart, and assign two helpers, one with a stopwatch and another to count steps. The fencer being tested will

stand facing away from the test area with her rear foot behind a line. The timer will command "go" and starts the watch, and stops the watch when the fencer's front foot crosses the second line. The other helper counts the number of rear foot movements that were made between the lines during the timing period. The objective is to cover the distance with as many steps as possible in the fastest time. Divide the number of steps by the time in seconds; the higher the number, the better. Short, fast steps will yield good scores.

Blade and Parry Exercises

5. Alternate changes of engagements are useful in learning to manipulate French foils with the fingers. One partner can remain stationary while the other makes several changes with light blade contact, or both partners can each in turn make circular changes which also reinforce the circle parry motions. Adding footwork will make the drill a bit more difficult since it requires coordinating the hand and feet.

6. To develop lightness, precision, and accuracy, do an alternating series of parries and ripostes with both partners staying on guard and slightly out of touch distance. Try to limit all movements to the foil arm without any leaning in or out. To make the drill more realistic, do the drill with continuous lunges and recoveries as each partner in turn parries during recovery and ripostes with a lunge. Neither partner should hit the other. More advanced fencers can choose to riposte directly or by disengagements or one-twos without any pre-arrangement as to which will be used.

7. To improve the ability to make small deceptive moves, one partner will stand with a fully extended arm while the other will make varying lateral and circular parry movements that the extended partner has to avoid through the use of minimal point travel. The parry movements should be purposely slow enough that they can be successfully deceived. Add footwork for more difficulty.

8. To practice simple deception attacks, play a game in which D has one line open as he stands against a wall and so cannot retreat. The attacker has the choice of making either a direct attack or a disengagement. D will try to parry only those actions that look real and will not parry if the attack is clearly a disengagement. To keep D from just guessing, A should make a few direct lunges that are sure to be parried before making an attack by means of a feint and disengagement. This is a great test of a fencer's ability to make convincing feints that will fool the opponent into parrying. Of course the touch must be delivered with a powerful lunge. The drill also

sharpens the defender's ability to distinguish between direct and poorly made indirect attacks.

9. The above drill can be modified to allow A to make *either* a direct, indirect, or a one-two attack, all only to one of the high lines. D is limited to using only lateral parries. In another variation, D can use only a circle six parry while A may make either direct lunges or doubles.

10. Practice the transitions between any of the four common parries (4, 6, 7, and 8) by having partner A stand with a fully extended arm aiming his foil at any line and holding it there until D completes and holds the proper parry. If no correction to the parry is needed, then A will aim at another line without ever flexing his arm. The objective is for D to learn to move precisely from parry to parry. There should be no lunging or attempting to actually touch. An advanced version of the drill involves an extended arm leader who may advance or retreat while the follower continues to parry while in motion.

11. Fencer D will stand with his point in line and will try to deceive A's attempts to beat. If the beat is successful, D will parry the attack that follows. Some of A's early beat movements should be purposely slow and obvious to encourage successful deception, but gradually A occasionally should make a very fast beat lunge to try to hit D before the attack can be parried.

To simplify matters, only the fourth beat should be used.

12. The defender will stand with an eighth invitation position and, when attacked, will either parry four or six or will take a step back without parrying at all. A riposte should follow a successful parry. Later, A may try to deceive the parry, or, if D retreats, may optionally recover forward and lunge again. The defender's unpredictability should give her the advantage.

13. This beat and disengage drill requires D to respond to A's beat by making a full lateral parry which A will deceive while lunging. As a variation, use an advance lunge, beating during the advance and deceiving during the lunge. The defender cooperates by delaying her parry until she has taken a step back.

Timing and Tactics

14. The timing of a counter attack can be improved by having partner A lunge and immediately recover while the defender D retreats once to avoid the attack and then lunges or advance lunges at the start of the A's recovery so as to hit before a full recovery can be completed. For advanced fencers, the drill may be modified by having the offensive partner make a designated number of advances while the defender retreats an equal number of times

to maintain distance. When the attacker does finally lunge, the defender makes just enough of an additional retreat to avoid that attack before launching his own counter attack. Any pre-arranged blade skill could be used by either partner.

15. To develop timing of attacks, the "teacher" A who is just out of distance will make a single advance with *either* a bent foil arm or with an extending foil arm. If A's foil arm is bent, then the "pupil" D should lunge just as A begins to advance, not after the advance is completed. But if there is a threatening extension by A, then D should retreat but not parry. Although it is natural to want to parry a potential threat, the drill should serve to encourage the use of retreats

    The same drill for more advanced students can be varied to permit D to do a beat parry and riposte when A steps forward with an extended arm.

16. A difficult but useful bouting drill is to have a designated defender and attacker with the defender agreeing to use only a specific parry, either one lateral or a circular parry six, in addition to the usual retreats. The attacker knowing ahead of time which parry will be used must try to judge the correct time and distance in order to deceive the parry and score a touch. The attacker can of course choose to make direct lunges instead of trying to deceive the parry in case the defender is either guessing or is not responding to feints. The defender is permitted to occasionally lunge to keep the attacker alert.

    You would assume that when you are playing the role of defender you are at a disadvantage, but that isn't necessarily true. You can still keep your distance and select when to use the designated parry or to not parry when the attacker's feint is unconvincing. Although the attacker knows which parry you will be using, he still has the very difficult tasks of making a perfectly executed deceiving skill and delivering the blade with an effective lunge. The drill makes clear how difficult it is to score a hit and that only a small percentage of attacks in a bout will result in touches.

17. For moderately advanced fencers, I have used a "no parry and no beat" bout in which the fencers are limited to using only retreats to avoid attacks and may not parry, make an advance lunge, nor have a point in line. As you "bout," some strategy emerges. You may find that a fake lunge can be effective to entice the opponent into counter-attacking when you are prepared to recover and make your own counter-attack. This is a form of second intention, and the difficulty is in resisting the natural tendency to parry. A referee can be used to disallow any touches that violate the rules for the drill. Since no parries may be used, there is no use for feints.

18. An interesting exercise is for two fencers to decide upon some choreographed phrase as might two actors practicing for a stage duel. Practice slowly at first, and repeat the routine until both are satisfied. Then gradually increase the speed of the phrase until it approximates bout speed. Start with a simple routine such as a direct lunge which is parried and as the attacker recovers with a circle six parry, the defender ripostes with a double and lunge. Possible routines and their complexities are limited only by the imagination and the skill levels of the partners.

Solo Drills

There are not many things you can do alone to improve your fencing. A wall target does have value in developing your lunge and accuracy. Try hitting the target with your blade originating from a different position each time, for example, with the tip near the floor, over your shoulder, or way out to the side. From any of these locations, without lunging, whip your point in line with the target, pause very slightly to assure your aim, then touch.

A full-length mirror can be useful in checking out your form either from a front view or from profile. You can also do some "shadow fencing" in front of the mirror using both offensive and defensive skills to see how you appear to an opponent.

You can improve the power and length of your lunge by placing some small, light object such as an empty can, in front of your front foot while you stand on guard. Start your lunge by swiftly kicking the object and otherwise lunging normally. The kick is made by almost fully extending the front knee; your heel will strike the floor first as the lunge is completed.

Games

▶ As a change of pace, some simple games can be played by members of a class. The children's game that I call "*hot hands*" is really a neat test of fencers' reaction times. One player stands with palms up and the partner places his hands on top, palms down. The down partner tries to slap one or both hands of the other who of course tries to avoid having his hand slapped. Successful avoidance results in a switch of positions.

▶ A *foot stomp* game starts with each partner placing his hands on the shoulders of the other with arms remaining fully extended throughout. Both keep their feet well back out of danger of being stomped upon, but when one invites by extending a foot into the center, the other will attempt to stomp it. Some strategy soon surfaces and the players try to lure (invite) the opponent into traps. No street shoes should be worn for this game.

▶ A test of balance and sense of strategy involves two players who stand almost toe to toe with feet together and hands held about shoulder height but not in contact. The objective is to cause the partner to move a foot or lose balance without touching any body part except the hands. A sharp push to the hands may cause the partner to fall backwards, and a yielding by the hands when the partner expects resistance may cause a forward loss of balance. Some hand feints can be employed.

▶ For youngsters in a class, the age-old Simon Says game can be a nice change from the usual footwork drills. Simon Says "lunge," Simon Says "advance," "retreat"—gotcha! Any such activities should last for only a few minutes so that the class will not become bored. Leave them wanting more. Even adults get a kick out of this game.

▶ Just for fun, try balancing your foil with its tip on the end of your finger. When you can do this successfully, try it while you are on guard and use advances or retreats while balancing the foil. You can even try to lunge and recover. If a class is doing this, be sure that everyone has plenty of space to move because eyes will be looking up and people may bump into one another.

▶ In a children's beginner class, I inflate a few balloons and have each child tap (not smack) a balloon upward with his or her foil to keep it from hitting the floor. The object is to teach some blade control and improve hand-eye coordination. If several children are drilling at once in a small area, they should have masks on.

Appendix D

Principles of Refereeing

I have done and seen enough refereeing over the years that I can offer some guidance to those embarking on an officiating path. Like most fencers at one time or another in their careers, you will be asked to referee a pool or two at some competition. This is always a daunting task and the best place to get your feet wet will be during informal club bouts where nothing is at stake if you make errors. Take advantage of every opportunity to referee (some still say direct) bouts, particularly electrically fenced bouts, and by all means observe rated referees in action and attend any training seminars you may hear about. If you wish to become a rated referee, log onto www.fencingofficials.org, a web site that has a downloadable study guide. You will have to take a written examination and then take a practical exam of your refereeing abilities under the watchful eye of a qualified examiner.

There are ten levels of rated referees. The entry level is ten, which qualifies the referee to work unclassified meets. As a nine, the referee can handle E level competitions, and so on up the scale to the very top referee rating of one.

Previously, the official in charge of a bout was known as the director and, in some places, the president. Whatever the title, the referee's most important and most difficult task is to determine right of way when lights on both sides of the scoring box come on during an action. In a heated bout with the score at 4–4, many referees hope that the last phrase of action will produce only a single colored light so that the burden of calling the priority is off the referee's shoulders. The French term "la belle" reflects that wish for a clean, beautiful hit to end a tied bout so there will be no disagreements.

Needless to say, as a referee you should know and be able to apply the current rules and terminology. What is the definition of an attack or of a parry? Some referees insist that the attacker's foil arm must be fully extended at the start of a lunge. Others view the rule differently and give priority to attacks in which the foil arm is *extending* while the foil tip is moving toward the target, which, by the way, is the current interpretation. What actions warrant a yellow, red, or black card?

Rules change occasionally and interpretations seem to change too often. The official rules are in French, and when changes are made there are often problems of translation or interpretation. To help achieve consistency of applying the rules, rated referees are currently required to attend seminars annually.

> ▶ ▶ ▶ I note that the 1957 Rules Book stated that "the rules do not require that the attack be made with a fully extended arm . . . ," implying that only a forward movement of the arm is needed to have the right of way. Interpretations do change periodically.

As a referee, you are in charge of bouts and your decisions about priority cannot be disputed. Accept the fact that every referee, you and me included, will make mistakes from time to time. That holds true for officials in any sport where quick judgments are expected. Spectators delight in shouting criticism at sports officials who, as in international soccer events, sometimes have to run for their lives at the end of a contest. Fortunately, such is not the case in our sport, but sometimes coaches, parents, and spectators can be harshly critical of a referee's calls. Remember that you can ask for quiet and even eject bystanders (by issuing a black card) who continue to give you verbal abuse after having been warned. But happily most people at the site will usually behave admirably and you will not have major problems.

Be firm but have a sense of humor when the fencers give you a hard time. A thick skin develops as you get experience in dealing with volatile fencers who disagree with every call against them. Do not permit arguments about matters within your discretion. Only questions regarding possible misapplications of rules are allowed. Also you have to learn to ignore gestures and comments by fencers or others who are trying to influence your decisions.

Fencing action is at least as fast as any found in other sports and being a referee is very difficult, especially when so many decisions have to be made over the course of a long competition. One positive outcome of doing some refereeing yourself is that it gives you an appreciation of how hard the job is, and you will be more tolerant when you are fencing and you receive some questionable calls.

In many local meets, you might have to referee a bout that involves one of your own teammates or even one that is within your own pool. Obviously, you are expected to be impartial in such situations. There is always a shortage of non-involved, competent referees at every level, even at national events. Officiating is generally a labor of love and takes many hours of a person's time for which there is seldom more than just token compensation.

Refereeing Procedures

As for the mechanics of refereeing, the routine is pretty cut and dried. The fencers will have hooked up to the reels and will come to your strip holding their foils vertically to allow you to place the test weight on the tips. A light tap downward will turn on the white light on the scoring box, and the tip spring must be able to push the weight back up thereby canceling the light. You give a yellow penalty card if a foil doesn't pass that test, and if the replacement foil also does not pass, the fencer receives a red card and the opponent is given a point.

It also happens that the foil is okay but the body cord is defective and the white light won't turn off. That too is a reason to give a penalty card. Fencers are responsible only for their own equipment. No penalty cards are given for any problems with the scoring equipment, reels, and cables.

Assuming that the weapons pass the tests, you should check each fencer to see that the body cord's alligator clip is attached on the rear of the lamé on the side of the weapon arm and that the body cord has a retaining device. If a prior mask test was done, look for the mark indicating that the mask passed the safety test. You will also make certain that the fencers are wearing underarm protectors and that uniforms conform to the rules.

The fencers should stand behind the on guard lines, salute one another, and salute you as required by the rules. You start the bout with the commands "on guard," "ready?" "fence." There are universal hand signals that accompany each of these verbal commands: palms down for "on guard," palms up for "ready?," and palms moving toward one another for "fence." Once the bout commences, the next word will be "halt" whenever the scoring box shows a light indicating a touch on or off the target. You may also stop the bout if you see a rules violation or some problem with equipment or clothing.

As a referee you must always be in position to see the scoring box lights as well as both fencers, and this requires considerable movement by you. You should focus on the blade action and place yourself to see the scoring box between the fencers. When a light comes on, immediately call a loud "Halt" and, in your mind, analyze the phrase. Determine which fencer had the initial priority and then sort out whether there were one or more parries and ripostes. This might be compared to viewing a TV instant replay of the action. Then, without hesitation, describe the phrase, announce your decision, and award the point. Delaying your call may

On guard!

Ready?

Play!

Halt!

Attack!/Counter-attack!

Simultaneous!

Point in line

Hit against!

Not valid!

Parried!

Hit scored for!

Figure 25. *Referee Hand Signals*

reflect on your competency. When both scoring lights are on and you cannot determine which of the fencers had priority, then say so quickly and resume the bout. It does happen that both fencers had equal priority and both touched. In that case you announce that the attacks were simultaneous and no point is awarded, even if one of the touches was off target.

Resist the temptation to give a detailed description of the fencing phrase because you might open the door to dispute. Rather, use only the defined fencing terms and the appropriate hand signals while briefly identifying the attack or the riposte and state your decision. When you analyze a phrase, the highest priority is given to a point in line. Next in rank order are an attack, a prise de fer, a riposte, a counter attack, and finally a remise or redoublement.

The fencers return to the on guard lines only if a point was awarded. In addition to watching for scoring lights, you have to be alert to possible violations such as a fencer covering the target area with the rear arm or stepping off the side of the strip.

> ▶ ▶ ▶ When no point is awarded, the fencers come on guard at a distance such that when they extend their arms, their foil tips will be point to point. Interestingly, this is the exact distance for two duelists as illustrated and described by Prevost in his 1891 book, *L'Escrime at Le Duel.*

Probably the single most difficult action to call is when one fencer is attempting to make a beat at the same instant that the other is attempting to parry or is also beating. You hear a single sound of blade contact and have no way of judging which one intended to beat and which meant to parry. It is very hard to identify intent, and, not being a mind reader, you might be justified in stating that you are unsure of who controlled the blade contact rendering priority doubtful. In such cases you have the point fenced over. I can tell you that it is often easier to referee a bout between two skilled fencers than between a couple of beginners because the actions of experienced fencers are usually more clear.

Another tough call for a referee is when a stop hit scores just before the arrival of the attacker's touch. By rule, a stop hit must actually land before the *start* of the final phase of an attack; otherwise it is just an incorrect counter attack into preparation. A good referee will make scoring decisions based on priority rather than on which light comes on first.

It is not unusual for a referee to have to also keep time and to record points on the score sheet, as well as make scoring decisions. That certainly makes it difficult to use hand signals, and it is always best to try to find a non-participant to keep score and time. If you can get such help, ask the person to call the current score out loud after each point that you award. That way any errors will be caught at once and disputes about the correct score will be avoided. You will help the scorekeeper and spectators by pointing in the direction of the priority and then by holding up your hand on the side of the fencer who scored along with stating verbally "touch right" or "touch left." Instruct the timer to yell halt when three minutes of fencing time have expired, and whoever was in the lead will be the bout winner. If, however, the score was tied at the end of fencing time, you will flip a coin and assign advantage to one fencer. The clock is reset and the bout will last another minute or to the first touch scored. If the score is still tied at the end of a minute, the victor is the fencer who had the advantage.

At the end of the pool, the referee should total the wins and losses and calculate the indicators on the official score sheet. The fencers will initial the score sheet and the referee will sign the sheet and turn it in to the bout committee.

Although most of the principles of refereeing are the same in all three weapons, there are some differences because of the rules that apply to each. The concept of priority is the same in foil and saber, but calling priority in saber is a bit more difficult because cuts as well as thrusts are used. With no priority as a concern in épée fencing, refereeing is perhaps easier, but there are rules specific to that weapon about which referees must be aware.

In conclusion, you should practice your refereeing skills often at fencing practices and, when you feel ready, at some novice level competitions. You can find the rules posted www.usfencing.org, but be aware of any changes made since those rules were posted.

> ▶▶▶ **Strip dimensions have changed numerous times over the years before finally settling on the current 14 meter strip length for all weapons. At various times, the strip length for the saber and épée had been 18 m or 24 m.**
>
> **Time limits have changed from 10 minutes to 6 to 4 to the present 3 for a five-touch bout. The current shorter time limit puts more emphasis on action and reduces tactical delays.**
>
> **At one time, women's foil bouts were fought to four touches and the lower edge of the target was the waist.**

Some Words about Non-Electric Fencing

In the "good old days" before the electric foil came into use in the mid 1950s, there was a sort of training ground for referees. All fencers had to participate in judging bouts and so had plenty of opportunities to closely observe referees at work. I believe that electric scoring has eliminated the intermediate step between being a fencer and becoming a referee. But none of us would want to return to using "dry" foils. It was tiring to have to both fence and judge and sometimes referee. There were many abstentions and inaccuracies in the voting because of the difficulties in seeing whether or where touches may have landed.

On the positive side, however, there was no expense for scoring boxes, reels, floor cords, metallic strips, lamés, electric foils, or body cords. Think of the time saved by not having to tape down or roll up the copper strips or to move heavy modular strips. Even today, there are places where non-electric competitions are still held, notably in college physical education classes that normally don't own electric equipment. The USFA website no longer provides the information needed to conduct such meets, and for that reason, I will summarize the major topics and rules needed to hold "dry" meets.

Judging

Instead of a scoring box, there are four judges, two on either side of the fencers. A judge's only duty is to watch for touches made on the fencer who is on the opposite end and facing the judge. Upon seeing any touch, on or off the target, a judge must raise a hand, which signals the referee to call a halt. The referee then reconstructs the phrase and polls the judges on the side of the fencer who was considered to have priority.

Each judge has four possible votes to cast when asked by the referee:

▶ The vote is Yes, if the touch was valid, that is, on the target,

▶ No, if there was no hit or the hit attempt was parried,

▶ Off Target, if the touch was on invalid target,

▶ Abstain, if the judge is uncertain or has no opinion.

Each judge's vote is worth one point and the referee's vote is worth one and a half points. If two judges on the same side cast the same vote, other than abstaining, their combined two points will prevail even if the referee has a different vote. But if one judge abstains, the referee's extra half point vote would be more than the other judge's one point vote if it disagrees with the referee. An abstention carries no point value, and if the judges and referee all abstain, it is ruled to be a "doubtful touch" and no point can be awarded. It is also a doubtful touch if the two judges disagree and the referee abstains.

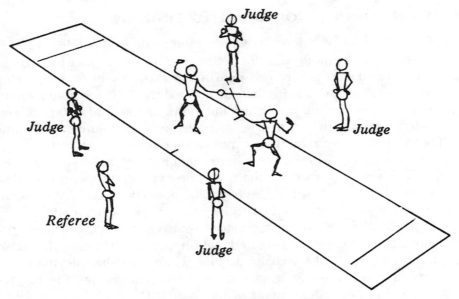

Figure 26. *Judging Positions for Non-Electric Bouts*

In effect, a judge is taking the role of one side of an electric foil scoring box and just gives a verbal vote in place of the scoring box showing a white or colored light. The referee's responsibilities for determining priority are the same as in electric foil bouts, but she has the additional responsibility of watching for touches in her role as a judge.

Since non-electric bouts do not require a metallic strip, the meet organizers normally lay out the strip boundaries and various lines on the gym floor using tape. I would caution you to use tape specially made for varnished floor surfaces because otherwise, the removal of the tape after the meet might pull up varnish with it. The gym owner or host school would naturally be upset about such floor damage, and your group will not be welcome again.

Votes					
Judge A (1 point)	*Judge B (1 point)*	*Referee (1 1/2 points)*	*Total Ballot Points*	*Decision*	*Point Awarded?*
Yes	Yes	Yes	3 1/2–0	Good touch	Yes
No	No	No	3 1/2–0	No touch	No
Yes	No	No	1–2 1/2	No touch	No
Yes	Yes	No	2–1 1/2	Good touch	Yes
No	No	Yes	2–1 1/2	No touch	No
Yes	Abstain	No	1–0–1 1/2	No touch	No
No	Abstain	Yes	1–0–1 1/2	Good touch	Yes
Yes	No	Abstain	1–1–0	Doubtful touch	No
Off Target	Abstain	No	1–0–1 1/2	No touch	No
Off Target	Abstain	Yes	1–0–1 1/2	Good touch	Yes
Off Target	Yes	No	1–1–1 1/2	Doubtful touch*	No
Off Target	No (or Yes)	Abstain	1–1–0	Doubtful touch	No
Off Target	Off Target	Yes (or No)	1–1 1/2	Off Target	No
Abstain	Abstain	Abstain	0–0–0	Doubtful touch	No
Yes	Abstain	Abstain	1–0–0	Good touch	Yes
No	Abstain	Abstain	1–0–0	No touch	No
Abstain	Abstain	No	0–0–1 1/2	No touch	No
Abstain	Abstain	Yes	0–0–1 1/2	Good touch	Yes

*The decision is doubtful touch because there is no majority view for any one vote. Even though the 2 judges disagreed with each other, they jointly differed with the referee.

Figure 27. *Voting Table for Non-Electric Bouts*

> ▶ ▶ ▶ **The use of judges is nothing new. Consider the fencing scene from Shakespeare:**
>
> **Hamlet: "One." Laertes: "No." Hamlet: "Judgement." Osric (the judge): "A hit, a very palpable hit."**

Self-Testing Questions

1. How many levels of referee ratings are there? Which is the highest rating?

2. What is the definition of a correct attack?

3. As a referee, what will you do if one of the fencer's foils fails your weight test?

4. Where should a fencer's body cord alligator clip be attached?

5. Which fencing action has the highest priority?

6. In non-electric foil fencing, if one judge votes yes, the other votes no, and the referee abstains, what is the decision?

7. Should the touch be allowed if a fencer scores with one foot off the side of the strip before the referee calls halt?

8. If time has expired with the fencers tied, what should the referee do?

9. What is the most common meet format?

10. If in a simultaneous attack one fencer is on target and the other off-target, what is the decision?

11. How many yellow cards can a fencer receive in any given bout?

12. How many red cards can a fencer receive in any given bout?

Appendix E

Conditioning— Are You Fit to Fence?

A s is true in all sports, the purposes of conditioning are to enhance performance and to minimize injuries to muscles, ligaments, or joints. There are no exercise programs that are unique to fencing, and even if there were, each individual is sufficiently different that no single program is suitable for everyone's needs. I don't believe in "one size fits all" exercise routines.

In this section I will describe some fundamental concepts with which every athlete, casual or advanced, should be familiar, and will suggest how these might apply to fencing. This topic is so complex and controversial that I will deal only with some generalities although I know that even these will not satisfy those who are strong advocates of particular approaches to fitness.

We all have both potentials and limitations that stem from genetic factors over which we have no control. Characteristics such as being tall or left-handed cannot be acquired or improved upon through exercise. Having inherent quick reaction time, an abundance of fast twitch muscle fibers, or exceptional flexibility are certainly advantages in fencing. If you are not so endowed, you can compensate somewhat by developing technically efficient movements and enhancing your overall physical condition.

I will go out on a shaky limb and state that the average recreational fencer does not need a formal conditioning program because fencing alone will improve fitness to some extent and the limited time most of you have at the salle should be devoted to fencing. As a physical educator, I have a strong belief that everyone needs daily exercise, but for the fencer this is better done at home or at a well-equipped gym where there are others to help with the motivation that might otherwise be lacking. Sometimes we all need to be pushed a bit. But there is a difference in goals between exercising and conditioning. Such activities as walking, shoveling snow, playing tennis, and roller-blading are forms of exercise. Conditioning can be said to go *beyond* exercise in that its aim is to help an athlete's ability to win.

Conditioning does not appeal to everyone and it takes considerable motivation to work out or to try to lose weight. That is why some are willing to pay personal trainers for help. For beginners who have been sedentary, fencing may be the only exercise needed to increase fitness levels. For aspiring competitive fencers, improvements in overall fitness through any conditioning program can contribute to success in the sport. If you are an A rated fencer with Olympic team goals, then you definitely need to work on achieving the highest possible degree of fitness.

What Is Fitness?

Are you fit? That question cannot be easily answered without first defining fitness. In a broad sense, fitness has the three components of strength, endurance, and flexibility and all of these are of importance in varying degrees in fencing. Each is quite specific to different areas of the body. For example, you might have very strong arms but relatively weak legs, or you might not be able to touch your toes but are very flexible in the shoulders. So what does an average fencer need to be fit, and how can condition be improved?

Perhaps a definition of fitness for fencing could be expressed in terms of how well a fencer can get through a pool or a couple of rounds of direct elimination without feeling exhausted. It is probably safe or even obvious to say that, other things being equal (are they ever?), the fencer who is physically the more fit is more likely to win. I believe that fitness contributes to self-confidence on the strip, and in daily life it is certainly a factor in overall well-being and self-esteem.

For the beginner or recreational fencer, assuming that there are no existing medical problems, fencing is a relatively safe sport and risk of injury to muscles or joints is minimal. If your on guard stance is correct, your knees will be directly over their respective feet and there will be no strain on the knee ligaments. Good form and footwork are anatomy-friendly, by which I mean that risk of injury is less if your movements conform to the way your joints are designed to function.

It makes sense to start an exercise program slowly because trying to do too much too soon could cause harm. Confer with your family physician about the need for a physical examination. Begin with a self-assessment by asking such obvious questions as: How fit am I right now? Do I have any problems that might preclude certain exercises, e.g., bad knees? Should I pursue an exercise program or a conditioning program? How much time am I willing and able to spend on such programs? Do I need to diet?

Flexibility

This is defined as the range of motion around a particular joint, so we cannot refer to a person as being flexible but rather must identify specific joints of interest. As fencers we should be concerned with the muscles and ligaments of the hip joints because of their obvious involvement in lunging. Those who are already flexible, as many women are, can concentrate on improving strength and endurance.

Increasing flexibility is a long process so don't expect quick, dramatic results, especially if you are an adult with a rather short lunge capability. First decide how much flexibility you need and then find out how to go about increasing it. Our flexibility is in large part related to our genes and is limited by the structure of our joints and the tightness of the surrounding muscles, tendons, and ligaments. We are not all built to be able to do splits.

There are numerous exercises that will stretch muscles and tendons around the hip joint. One example is shown in figure 28 in which a leg is first raised to a vertical position and then crossed over at close to a right angle to the body. From the elevated position, allow gravity to bring your leg down while you relax the resisting muscles. This puts a stretch on the hamstrings, the buttock muscles, and the iliotibial band located on the outside of the thigh.

Figure 28. *A Cross-Over Stretch*

To increase flexibility you must apply the principle of **overload,** that is, you must move a body part to its present limit and then gently go an inch or two beyond and hold it there in order to put a stretch on the ligaments, tendons, and muscles around the joint. There is no consensus as to how long to hold the stretch, but I would guess that it should be twenty to thirty seconds long. There should be some discomfort, but if you experience pain, you have gone too far.

To work toward achieving a longer lunge, take the longest lunge position that you can and move your lead foot forward an inch or so and hold it there. This is called "**static stretching**" and it can be done in two ways. It is labeled "**active**" when the individual is moving the body part, and it is "**passive**" if someone else is assisting in the movement. Passive static stretching does produce a greater range of motion, but there is the risk that the assisting person can push or pull too far or too fast and cause injury.

In what is termed "**ballistic**" or bounce stretching, the momentum generated is hard to control and might cause tissue tear. An example of ballistic stretching is in toe touching from an erect position wherein a person reaches down, slightly withdraws, and then forcefully bends a bit further. This forced elongation of tissue does work but also puts hundreds of pounds of force on the vertebrae of the lower back. You can more safely achieve the desired result of stretching the hamstring muscle group by sitting on the floor with legs extended, reaching for your toes, and holding the position statically.

Another area of concern for fencers is the Achille's tendon located behind the ankle just above the heel. That tendon connects the calf muscles to the back of the heel. Stretching the calf muscles before fencing may help to reduce the possibility for a rupture of that most important tendon. The common exercise to stretch the calf muscles (gastrocnemius and soleus) is illustrated in figure 29.

Figure 29. *One Method of Calf Muscle Stretch*

Another common stretch is illustrated in figure 30 in which you would start in a wide straddle position with the feet parallel. Move your torso to the right and press your weight down until you feel tension on the inside of your left thigh (the adductor muscles). Hold the position for a half-minute and then do the same in the other direction. This is similar to a lunge position except that both feet face forward.

Some people report that yoga and Pilates programs are very helpful in improving joint flexibility. Regardless of the program you choose to follow, be careful to not overstretch and cause more harm than good. Reasonable policies to follow in all of your conditioning efforts are: "everything in moderation" and "listen to your body."

Any stretching that you might do before a fencing practice or competition might have a warm up benefit for the leg muscles but will not increase range of motion long term. I don't know of any formula for determining how much warm up stretching is needed before fencing or to what extent such stretching has even been proven to prevent injury. But theories abound and you should do what feels best to you.

Figure 30. *An Adductor Muscle Stretch*

Strength

Strength is defined as the ability of a muscle or muscle group to move some maximal weight *one time*. For example, a competitive weight lifter has to raise a barbell just once. How much strength does a fencer require and which muscle groups are most involved? Again the key word to improvement is overload, and gains in strength come from gradually adding more weight than you can presently lift or move. Foils are not heavy and so the arms and shoulders don't have to be particularly strong. Grip strength is helpful in fencing and can be improved through the regular use of various squeezing devices or rubber balls.

Muscles can be exercised either **isometrically** or **isotonically,** the former meaning that the muscle is attempting to contract against some resistance but no motion results, and in the latter, the muscle's contraction produces movement. Standing on guard requires an isometric contraction of, for example, the muscles on the front of the thighs, the quadriceps. When lunging, those same muscles contract isotonically to extend the knee joint of the rear leg. Being on guard with your point in line requires an isometric contraction of the shoulder muscles.

A well-known isometric exercise to improve the chest muscles is done by placing palms together and pushing very hard for a few seconds, rest and repeat several times. Or, for the rear shoulder muscles, lock fingers at chin level and pull hard. You can easily incorporate both isometric and isotonic contractions into a single exercise as, for instance, lifting a small weight out to the side, holding it there for a few seconds, and slowly lowering it. The main advantage of isometrics is that they can be done anywhere and don't require equipment, but they can be boring and strength gains take time.

It is generally accepted that isotonic exercises are more effective than are isometric because they move body parts through a full range of motion. Isotonic contractions are of two types—**concentric** and **eccentric.** A concentric contraction occurs when a muscle shortens to cause movement as when you do a chin up. In an eccentric contraction, the muscle lengthens against some resistance to allow movement. When you lower your body after a chin up you are using an eccentric contraction of the same muscles that had lifted you.

Shallow knee bends and vertical jumps will help to improve the strength of the hip and knee extender muscles which are so important in fencing, but overload is needed if there is to be a substantial strength increase. That could involve holding some weight while doing the knee bends or jumps. Exercise rubber tubing or stretch bands are inexpensive and can be used to tone the arm and leg muscles, both isometrically and isotonically. Of course there are various exercise machines designed specifically to develop arm or leg strength.

Strength development also benefits the tendons and ligaments and has many approaches. An exercise can be done faster, longer, with more resistance, or with reduced resting time between sets. There are guide lines that are widely accepted such as **progressive training** wherein a particular weight is lifted repeatedly until it can be done perhaps ten or twelve times to failure, which is referred to as a *set*. After a rest of about three minutes, repeat the set. If a set becomes too easy, then you should increase the resistance.

Any strenuous exercise should be done only every other day to give the muscles some rest and time to repair. Muscle balance is important—if you exercise muscles that flex a joint, you should spend time to also work on the muscles that extend (flexing is bending at a joint, extending is straightening).

If you are planning to lift heavy weights, be sure to use good form to avoid tearing muscles, injuring the back or developing a hernia. Finally, strong muscles are the first lines of defense against joint injury, and in fencing it is the knee joint that needs the protection given by well-developed flexor and extensor muscles.

> ►►► Hundreds of muscles are used in fencing actions, but the major leg muscles that a fencer might want to develop include:
>
> Calf muscles—Gastrocnemius and soleus which "plantar flex" the foot, i.e., point it downward.
>
> Knee extensors—The four muscles comprising the quadriceps femoris are on the front of the thigh.
>
> Hip extensors—The three muscles comprising the so-called hamstrings are on the back of the thigh.

Endurance

Here we can discuss the endurance of specific muscle groups or of the cardio-respiratory system. **Muscle endurance** is defined as the ability of a muscle or muscle group to contract repeatedly against some less than maximal resistance. For instance, moving rapidly up and down the strip, doing pullups, pushups, or situps are all isotonic exercises requiring muscular endurance.

Pushups are excellent exercises for fencers, but if you find pushups to be too difficult, try modified pushups by placing your hands on the edge of a table or sturdy chair.

Good abdominal muscle tone is important for all activities. The "abs" can be exercised by several means, some requiring equipment and some not. Everyone has at some time done situps, but it is generally considered best to do **crunches.** Lie on your back and with your arms either crossed in front of your chest or your hands loosely clasped behind your neck. Your knees should be well bent or even held straight up. Lift your head and shoulders just clear of the floor, then lower. Do as many as you can and do not pull on your neck.

Figure 31. *Modified Pushups*

Cardio-respiratory endurance refers to the heart and lungs and their capacity for sustaining activity over a long period of time. If you are huffing and puffing after a bout, you probably need to work on this aspect of your fitness. Being winded or having a fast heart beat after a very exerting activity is normal, but is not to be expected after a few minutes of casual fencing which, after all, involves only brief periods of intense movement and is not truly aerobic.

Both muscular and cardio-respiratory endurance can be improved by means of the overload principle. If you can do only six push ups, try for seven. If you can jog only one block without being pooped, next time try for a bit longer run. If you are having difficulty in running any distance, try to figure out which system is limiting your ability to run farther. It is possible that you have good leg muscular endurance but lack the needed cardio-respiratory endurance or vice versa. Both

Figure 32. *The Crunch*

types are needed, and you might try **interval training** that typically takes the form of jogs interspersed with short sprints. With at least a day's rest in between runs, you can follow one of two paths. You may try to increase distance while continuing to run or jog at the same speed, or you can increase your run speed for a given distance. A stopwatch is a great motivator as is a daily log of your workouts.

An excellent activity for any fencer is rope jumping which will develop the light footwork so necessary in fencing, along with cardio-respiratory endurance. A good rope is inexpensive and portable, and jumping can be done anywhere, preferably on a resilient floor. A downside to skipping rope is that, unlike other exercises, it requires some skill to be able to sustain jumps long enough to derive aerobic benefits. Of course, it is possible to just simulate the skipping without using a rope and not worry about the skill, but that could be boring. The correct rope length is important. When you stand on the center of the rope, the handles should reach your armpits.

It is obviously an advantage to be able to lunge with explosiveness and there are numerous approaches to developing **power,** especially leg power. Programs such as stair climbing, bounding, or plyometrics are useful for advanced fencers so long as they are done under the guidance of a trainer because there is always a risk to the knees even for fit athletes.

> ▶▶▶ **Power is the rate of doing work. Vertical jumps and standing long jumps are common tests of a person's power. Given two athletes of the same weight, the one who can run up a flight of stairs fastest is said to have the greater leg power.**

To somewhat relieve the boredom of too much exercise, try cross training a couple of times a week by playing basketball, swimming, tennis, or any other sport that you enjoy. Be concerned not only with your fitness for fencing but your overall well-being. Motivation can be improved by exercising with others and by writing down your week's fitness goals along with keeping a daily log of what you have done to achieve your goals.

Whether you are working on flexibility, strength, or endurance, your objective is to exceed your current abilities but never to the point of pain or nausea. There are no shortcuts. Set a realistic goal for yourself and stick to it. You may not see results for months, which is why so many people give up their programs or seek help from personal trainers. Benefits will be minimal if you exercise only one day a week; you have to find a way to set aside more time.

If you are middle-aged or older, be sure to get a physical and advice from your doctor before you embark on a vigorous exercise program. For those of you who may be approaching middle-age, I might mention that the aging process normally results in a diminution of physical abilities, but if you simply maintain the same level of activity over the years, you will in effect be offsetting the expected decline. In other words, if you have achieved a satisfactory fitness level, there may not be any need to get any stronger or to increase endurance or flexibility because, just by holding to current levels, you are balancing the normal losses that are experienced by those who do not exercise. From my point of view, this translates to the equivalent of increased fitness.

There is seemingly no end to the number of commercial devices advertised or programs offered to sell you products that range from useless to useful but expensive. Any bookstore or library will have many shelves of books that promise flat abs, firm buns, quick weight loss and so on, usually in just a few painless minutes a day. All I can say is that there are no fast and easy ways to achieving fitness and you can accomplish a lot without spending much. Finding a program that you enjoy is important if you are to persevere. Of course there are other considerations in achieving optimum performance. A sensible diet, weight control, and sufficient sleep are essential elements.

While any exercise can have some benefit, be careful that you do not delude yourself into thinking that you are really conditioning yourself. For instance, bicycling will increase endurance only if you pedal rapidly or seek out hills to climb. Similarly, swimming many laps slowly is not equivalent to fewer laps swum at full speed. Walking is excellent but brisk walking or going up stairs is better. Running short sprints is a valuable exercise but be sure to wear good shoes and try to do your running on a pliant surface such as a school track. As was said earlier, you don't have to invest a lot of money on fitness equipment.

Appendix F
Teaching Methodology

There are two basic formats for teaching fencing. Experienced teachers working with advanced students generally use **individual lessons,** while **group instruction** is the usual choice for teaching beginners. This section will deal with how an instructor can work with classes of beginning or intermediate level students.

In addition to college or high school physical education classes, fencing instruction is often available in city recreation programs, private agency programs, or fencing clubs' programs. Each of these situations requires different objectives and teaching methodologies. School programs usually involve some sort of testing and grade submissions, whereas courses elsewhere are largely recreational in nature and involve a wide range of participants' ages. Class sizes can vary from just a few students to as many as thirty. The number of students that can be accommodated in a program is usually limited by the amount of available equipment, the size of the room, and the instructor's capabilities. In some situations space is a luxury and a shortage of equipment might require some sharing by the students.

While this section is primarily directed to instructors of university or high school fencing courses, the content, with minor adaptations, can be of use in other settings as well. Any experienced teacher or coach of fencing has undoubtedly developed an efficient method for teaching classes, and I will not presume that my methods are in any way better. But for those who could benefit from my ideas and who are using this text in class, I will describe the approach to course planning and class organization that I have used over the years.

Initial Considerations in Planning

When preparing a course outline there are some obvious questions that must be answered before any lesson plans or course objectives can be drawn up:

1. How many times will the students be meeting and what is the length of the class?

2. How large will the class be and is there enough equipment and space for that number?

3. What is the probable motivation of the students? For instance, are they required to take this course or is it elective? Are the students serious about becoming competitors or will most be taking lessons for exercise and recreation?

4. What are the ages of the students? A children's class will require different planning than one for adults.

5. Will there be a follow-up opportunity when this session ends? If the course is terminal, then planning should be based on the class's short-term needs.

6. In a school setting, will grades have to be submitted and how will evaluation be done? How much time must be allotted for this?

7. If you as the instructor are not confident and experienced in teaching fencing to groups, then try to limit class size and the number of skills you will include. There is a small element of risk in fencing, so a teacher has to make special efforts to insure safe practices. Make every effort to get advice and read the first chapters of this book.

Based on the answers to the above questions, course objectives and a lesson plan draft can then be prepared starting with a list of the skills that can be effectively covered in the time frame. Regardless of the length of the course, there should be an allowance of time for doing some bouting and in some cases for student evaluation. For an instructor with a limited fencing background, it would be prudent to simply follow the skill sequences exactly as laid out in chapters 2 and 3. That content is sufficient for beginners enrolled in an average course of six to ten weeks. Longer courses, especially with serious students, would certainly include the material in later chapters and the drills in appendix C.

For a short course of, say, six or seven meetings, the minimal skills to be included from chapters 2 and 3 would be everything through the parry and riposte with some fencing time scheduled on the last day. In courses of perhaps eight to ten sessions, add the deceptive attacks and the circle parry six along with some basic strategies found in chapter 4. Lesson plans should be flexible enough so that skills can be added or removed according to the ability of the students to absorb the material. It is best to have the class learn a few skills well than to cover more material than can be mastered in the available time.

Typical Learning Patterns

In any class in any activity there will be a wide range of coordination and comprehension levels. The teacher understands this and plans accordingly. Some students will be naturally athletic while others will struggle with learning even the most basic movements. Where possible, the teacher could group students by ability but generally she has to work with the class as a whole.

Initial instruction will produce fairly rapid progress since the large muscle locomotor skills are not difficult to acquire. When blade drills are introduced, coordination differences between students become more apparent. The gap between the gifted and the less-gifted students becomes wider as more skills are taught. The longer the course, the more one sees individual styles emerge and that is acceptable so long as such variations do not stray too far from the norm.

Class Formations

There are four basic formations that I use when instructing a large group.

▶ The **single line** is used least because the students in a large class are so spread out that it is difficult for those on either end to hear and see. I use it when I do a leader-follower footwork drill with myself as the leader. It helps to have left-handed students to the right end of the line so that they can see the instructor more easily.

▶ The **single circle** is very good for instructing a new skill since everyone is the same distance from the teacher. It is a good formation for introducing such basic chapter 3 skills as the foil grip, salute, on guard, advance, retreat, and lunge.

▶ The **double circle** is best for demonstrating and practicing paired partner drills such as the hit, the lunge at a partner, parrying, riposting, etc.

▶ Finally the **double line** formation is used when a drill requires pairs to be moving.

Regardless of the formation used, in all paired activities, students should always play the role of teacher for their partners. Teach the class to observe and correct any errors that may be made by their drill partners.

In the following sample course outline, the teacher should continuously refer back to the appropriate chapters in the book where more detailed descriptions are given for the various skills than are given below. Experienced teachers can of

There are a few common formations and methods for grouping the students. Each has its value for specific stages.

1. Single line:

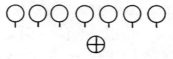

This is a good formation for initial instruction in footwork and lunging. Left-handers should be to the instructor's right.

2. Double line of paired partners:

This is the most common and useful formation both for teaching and early bouting. It permits easy rotation of partners.

3. Circle of paired partners:

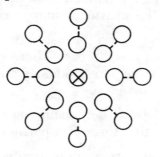

This has the advantage of centrally locating the instructor when a new blade skill is being taught. Rotation of partners is simple.

Figure 33. *Sketches of Four Basic Class Formations*

course present skills in any order of their choosing. This outline is for a physical education class but can certainly also be used in teaching any non-school situation.

Outline for a course which will meet for 9 to 12 forty-five-minute periods:

Day One: Take roll, pass out syllabi, fill out waivers, and explain the objectives in a fencing bout, the target area, the number of touches required to win, the strip length, how electrical fencing is conducted, etc. If the students are to select masks and jackets today, allow a lot of time for this if the class is large.

Day Two: No equipment is needed today. Have the students form a large single circle around the instructor who will demonstrate and have the class try the on guard position, the advance, the retreat, and the lunge. Next, have the students get into the single line formation in which they will follow the teacher in a leader-follower footwork drill. Then they will pair off and move into a double line formation in which they will again do a footwork drill with one line designated as the leaders. They are instructed to act as teachers for their partners and to make continual corrections in form.

Day Three: From the single circle formation, begin with a review, particularly for the benefit of added students. A bit of safety instruction is given and then only foils are passed out. The grip, the correct guard stance, and arm positions are covered, and the lunge is shown in three distinct actions: the arm extension, the lunge, and the recovery. Move the students into a single line and the teacher leads in more footwork review while the class tries to maintain correct positioning of the foil during movement. Those skills form the foundation of all that will follow.

Day Four: Jackets and masks are worn for the first time. If the foil blades are fairly flexible, very few women in class will express discomfort with being hit by thrusts. The jackets are usually padded, but plastrons or plastic chest protectors should be available for use by anyone who needs added padding.

The double circle formation works well for introducing the hit or thrust because all students are within easy view of the teacher who can make corrections without having to walk more than a few steps from one pair to another. Once the hit has been practiced, the class works on blade manipulation by doing a change of engagement drill. Positions four and six are shown next.

Still on the fourth day, the all-important lunge at a partner is introduced. For this and many of the other skills, have the class work on a teacher-pupil basis. They engage in fourth and when one partner moves her blade to the sixth position to expose her inside high line, her partner will extend, lunge, and remain in the lunge while form corrections are made. The teaching partner is told to look for the common errors in lunging: the rear knee did not extend, the rear foot did not remain flat on the floor, the lead foot did not point straight forward, or the rear arm did not swing. Lunges should be practiced at different distances. Remember that a light touch is all that is needed. Have the students on the inside of the circle move one partner clockwise and repeat the exercise. Frequent rotation is desirable so that everyone gets to practice with a variety of partners.

Day Five: After the usual review, the students pair off in a double line and do a leader-follower drill. The leader will advance or retreat a few times with blades engaged in fourth and will then stop and expose his target which is the cue for the follower to lunge. Corrections are made before the recovery and resumption of footwork. Have everyone change partners periodically and do so for all remaining class periods.

Day Six: Next on the agenda are the lateral parries four and six which are the only ones needed in a short course. Those are followed by instruction in the riposte and an explanation of right of way. Some elementary bouting may be done once the parry and riposte and the concept of priority have been taught. Note that in many drills, students engaged blades in order to control the drill. By contrast, when bouting, students should not engage blades.

Day Seven: A thorough review of all the skills, terminology, and basic rules can be followed by more practice fencing. Instruct partners to be on guard in sixth position so that each has a target exposed to direct attacks (they will not have as yet learned to deceive parries).

Day Eight: Judging procedures for non-electric fencing can be covered and everyone should have some practice at refereeing and judging. Divide the class into groups of seven (four judges, a referee, and two fencers). Bouts should be short, say three total touches, followed by rotations of positions and duties so that each student has an opportunity to referee.

An alternative experience, which involves no officiating, is a format wherein the class is divided into groups of five to seven students. Two will fence while the rest of the group is in a line waiting their turns. Each "bout" is fenced for a single touch, and the fencer who is touched will step to the end of the line and the winner stays up. It is up to the person who was hit to acknowledge the touch, as there are no judges. If there is any doubt about a touch or the priority if both fencers touched, it should simply be fenced over. With small groups, the teacher could arbitrate as needed.

Day Nine and Beyond: The next group of skills to be taught in order are the counter-riposte, advance lunge, disengagement, one-two, circle parry six, and the double. Assign the reading of the text's coverage of those skills and the appropriate chapters on strategies and drills.

The above outline does not include time for warm-ups or stretching because class time is best devoted to the skills and early lessons are not particularly strenuous. Of course instructors will make their own judgments about including exercises.

Where grades are required, prepare a short objective written examination, multiple choice and/or true-false, covering rules and fencing terminology based on assigned readings. Next, develop a plan to rate students' skills. I do not evaluate officiating abilities of students. My skill evaluation is based only on *quality* of performance, not on competitive results. I rate each student on form, footwork, lunge, offensive skills, and defensive skills *while they fence*. In a smaller class of perhaps twelve or less, I would probably evaluate one student at a time but that is not practical for larger classes. The skill scores are added to the written final exam scores to determine course grades.

In a private club setting, classes are normally small, can run forty-five minutes to an hour, and of course no evaluations for grading are needed. With small numbers more material can be covered per period than outlined above. Fitness levels of older students have to be taken into consideration to avoid muscle aches, and some class time can be used for flexibility and conditioning exercises. Children are usually enthusiastic and animated and are fun to teach, but they want to fence right away and are not too concerned about form and fundamentals. It takes a lot of patience by the teacher to handle and guide a children's class, but the results can be very rewarding.

Material in this chapter has centered on class situations. Experienced teachers, time permitting, may give individual lessons before, during, or after class. Teaching methodology for such lessons differs considerably from that used for group instruction and is beyond the scope of this book.

Equipment Concerns

Storage of equipment is a major problem. A teacher is fortunate if there is a storeroom dedicated to fencing where jackets can be hung and aired between classes. (For non-school courses, I have often had to tote a couple of duffle bags of equipment to class.) Arrangements must be made for the laundering of jackets every few periods.

Jackets and masks should be numbered so that students will be able to easily get the same items each time they come to class. I also mark sizes on the jackets and masks with an S, M, L, or XL to help in the initial selection process. For large classes, the use of half-jackets might be considered because they will fit a wide range of student sizes. Even though such jackets have only one sleeve, they still provide adequate protection to beginners who will not be doing a lot of fencing. Refer to appendix A for equipment suggestions.

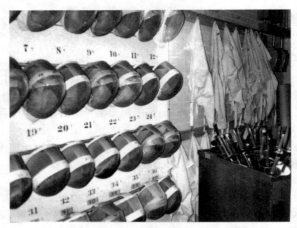

One Method of Storing Equipment

As for foils, I use a magic marker to put an X on the top surface of each blade just in front of the bell and in line with the top of the French handle. That makes it easier for students to find the handle top during the first couple of lessons. I mark the left-handed foils with a large L on the bell.

Summary

Class organization and lesson planning for fencing is pretty much the same as it would be for the teaching of any sport activity. Determine your objectives, estimate how much material can be covered in the allotted time, and consider the types of students who will take the course.

Skill presentation will be by the usual method of explanation, demonstration, practice, and further demonstration as needed. **Safety** is a primary concern and the teacher must always be present during class and alert to potentially dangerous actions by students.

Teachers using this book can of course arrange the order of the numbered skills to suit their needs. Assigning readings will save a lot of class time since it reduces the amount of lecturing that would otherwise be necessary. Maximize the time for skill acquisition and use those drills in appendix C that are appropriate for the level of your students.

I would encourage inexperienced teachers to read all available fencing books, some which are listed in Selected References. I also advise taking instruction from local fencing masters, observing competitions, attending any clinics that may be available, and utilizing the resources that can be found on the web site for the United States Fencing Association, www.usfencing.org. In one of your fencing classes may lurk a potential Olympian and you can take credit for starting her off. But you and all the average students will find that both you and they will have enjoyed the experience of learning to fence. Good luck.

Selected References

Alaux, Michel. *Modern Fencing*. New York: Charles Scribner's Sons, 1975.

Beke, Zoltan and Jozsef Polgár. *The Methodology of Sabre Fencing*. Budapest: Corvina Press, 1963.

Cass, Eleanor Baldwin. *The Book of Fencing*. Boston: Lothrop, Lee & Shepard Co., 1930.

Castello, Hugo and James. *Fencing*. New York: The Ronald Press. 1962

Castello, Julio. *The Theory and Practice of Fencing*. New York: Charles Scribner's Sons, 1933.

Castle, Egerton. *Schools and Masters of Fencing*. York, PA: George Shumway, 1969.

Cohen, Richard. *By the Sword*. New York: Random House, 2002.

Crosnier, Roger. *Fencing With the Foil*. London: Faber and Faber, 1951.

Deladrier, Clovis. *Modern Fencing*. Annapolis: United States Naval Institute, 1948.

Lukovich, Istvan. *Electric Foil Fencing*. Budapest: Corvina Press, 1971.

Morton, E.D. *A-Z of Fencing*. London: Queen Anne Press.

Nadi, Aldo. *On Fencing*. New York: G. P. Putnam's Sons, 1943.

Selberg, Charles. *Foil*. Reading, MA: Addison-Wesley Publishing Co., 1976.

Simonian, Charles. *Basic Foil Fencing*. Dubuque: Kendall/Hunt Publishing, 2005.

Szabó, László. *Fencing and the Master*. Budapest: Franklin Printing House, 1982.

Vass, Imre. *Épée Fencing*. Budapest: Corvina Press, 1965.

Glossary

Absence of Blade—Any position in which blades are not engaged.

Abstain—In non-electric fencing, the vote given when a judge has no opinion.

Acknowledgment—A declaration by a fencer that he or she was touched.

Advance—A forward step toward an opponent.

Advance Lunge—A combination of an advance and a lunge.

Armorer—A person who maintains and repairs electric scoring equipment.

Arret—French for stop hit, a thrust into an attacker's preparation which lands before the attacker's priority is established.

Allez—In French, referee's command to start fencing.

Attack—The initial offensive action in which the weapon arm is extending with the point threatening valid target.

Balestra—An attack made by a jump and lunge.

Barrage—A fence-off between fencers who are tied for some rank.

Beat—A sharp blow to an opponent's blade to gain priority or create an opening.

Bind—One form of prise de fer involving constant contact to deflect a point in line and carry it diagonally, usually from a high to a low line.

Black Penalty Card—The most severe penalty; it results in expulsion from a competition.

Bout—A competition between two fencers.

Bout Committee—A group responsible for conducting a competition including setting up the venue, seeding and assigning fencers to pools, determining results, and ruling on protests.

Circle Parry (or Counter Parry)—A circular parry in which the attacking blade is carried into a line opposite to that being threatened by the attack.

Closed Line—An engagement of blades which protects one's line of engagement from a direct attack.

Compound Attack—One which consists of two or more blade movements (e.g., a one-two or a double).

Corps-à-Corps—Physical contact between two fencers, usually penalized by a yellow card on the first occurrence.

Counter Attack—An attack into an attack or made immediately after opponent's attack failed.

Counter Riposte—An offensive action following a parry of the opponent's riposte.

Croisé—(French the cross) Generally is made after a parry to carry the attacker's blade to another line but on the same side as the parry.

Cutover—(French coupé) A form of disengagement made by passing one's blade over the opponent's blade into the opposite line.

Deceive—Also called a disengagement and is generally an avoidance of an opponent's parry drawn by a convincing feint of an attack.

Dérobement—(French) The avoidance of an opponent's attempt to attack or deflect one's blade, often when it is in line.

Direct Elimination—A tournament format wherein fencers are seeded after pools have ended. Bouts are fought to 15 touches within 9 minutes, and losing fencers are eliminated while winners advance one level.

Disarm—Loss of control of one's weapon which causes the referee to call a halt. There is no penalty and the fencer is given time to pick up the dropped weapon.

Disengagement—An attack in which the blade passes under the defender's weapon into another line (see deceive).

Double—A compound attack made by a direct or indirect feint followed by a circle to deceive the defender's circle parry (may also be pronounced doo-blay).

Double Touch—The referee's judgment that both fencers landed simultaneously. In foil and saber no point is awarded, but in épée each fencer receives a point.

Engagement—Any sustained contact of blades when neither fencer is attacking or defending.

Épée—One of three competitive weapons. Valid target is the entire body.

Escrime—The French word for fencing.

Esquive—(French) A term to describe any body evasive tactics to avoid an attack.

False Lunge—Usually a purposely short lunge intended to observe an opponent's reaction.

Feint—A blade action that is intended to resemble a threat and draw a reaction from the opponent.

Fencing Time—The time required to perform a single fencing action; may also be called tempo.

F.I.E.—The intials of the Federation Internationale d'Escrime, the world governing body for fencing.

Flèche—(French for arrow) An attack made by crossing the rear leg in front of the leading leg and often followed by a short run.

Flick—A cutover-like attack which arcs the blade downward to attempt to touch as opposed to a normal thrusting action.

Flunge—A saber attack in which a lunge is followed by a hop onto the leading foot; it may be used as a substitute for the flèche which is illegal in saber fencing.

Foible—The weaker forward portion of the blade.

Forte—The stronger portion of the blade near the bell.

Gainer Lunge—Also called an inverse lunge. The rear foot is brought close to the front foot and is followed by a lunge.

Indicator—A number determined by subtracting the total number of touches scored against a fencer in a pool from the total number the fencer scored against the opponents. The figure is used in ranking and seeding fencers into the next round or for resolving ties.

Infighting—Combat at close quarters which is permitted so long as there is no body contact and the referee can follow the action.

Inquartata—(Italian) A side stepping movement intended to avoid an attack.

Invitation—Any deliberate exposure of a target intended to entice an opponent to attack.

Judge—In non-electric foil this person's duty is to watch for touches on a fencer, and in electric fencing a judge may be assigned to look specifically for a violation such as the covering of target.

La Belle—(French for the beautiful) Sometimes used when a score is 4–4 and the referee hopes that the deciding touch will be so clear that there will not be any controversy.

Lamé—A conductive metallic vest worn over the jacket in electric fencing to cover the valid target.

Line—Usually refers to a target area such as high, low, inside, or outside. May also be used as a shortened form of "point in line."

Lunge—A means of reaching an opponent by moving the leading foot forward while the rear foot remains in place.

Maitre d'armes—(French) Also Master or Maestro. A teacher who is certified by passing the various accrediting examinations of a national coaches' association.

Match—The aggregate of the bouts fenced between members of two teams.

Modern Disengage—An attack in which a feint is made and followed by a withdrawal of the arm to deceive the opponent's parry. The arm is then re-extended to touch in the newly opened line.

N.C.A.A.—Initials of the National Collegiate Athletic Association.

Off Target—In foil, any touch with the point on an invalid target area.

On Guard—(French en garde) The normal stance of a fencer.

One-Two—A compound attack consisting of two deceiving actions or disengagements.

Opposition—An attacking or riposting action in which a blade or bell contact blocks out an opponent's weapon.

Parry—A blade action used to deflect an attack; may be lateral, circular, or semi-circular.

Pass—A crossing of one leg ahead of or behind the other in advancing or retreating.

Passata Soto—(Italian) An avoidance of an attack by ducking; generally made with a rear lunge and the unarmed hand placed on the floor for support.

Phrase—Any unbroken series of offensive and defensive blade actions.

Piste—(French) Another name for the fencing strip.

Point in Line—A defensive stance in which the weapon and arm form a straight line with the point threatening valid target.

Pointe d'arret—(French) The tip of a weapon, notably the tip of a non-electric épée.

Pool—A meet format in which a group of fencers will fence one another in a round robin manner.

Preparation—Any forward movement by a fencer who has not yet begun an attack and is therefore vulnerable to a stop hit or counter attack.

Prêt—(French for ready) When stated as a question, asks the fencers if they are ready to fence; otherwise it alerts the fencers that the next command will be "fence."

Priority—The right of way in a foil or saber bout given to the first fencer to initiate a proper attack or to riposte after a successful parry. The referee's primary task is to establish priority when both fencers touch during a phrase.

Prise de Fer—A generic term for any offensive blade action made with constant contact to control or divert an opponent's blade, as for example, a bind.

Pronation—A fencing hand position or parry in which the palm is turned down.

Recovery—The return from a lunge to an on guard position. May be in a forward or backward direction.

Red Penalty Card—Given by the referee as a penalty for a second infraction of the rules in a bout and results in a point to the opponent.

Redoublement—A new action made immediately after a failed original attack.

Referee—The official in charge of a bout; formerly called the director or president.

Remise—A continuation of an original attack which was parried but goes on to touch without a bending of the weapon arm or seeking a new target.

Retreat—A step backward from an opponent to maintain distance or to avoid an attack.

Right of Way—Another term for priority used to determine which fencer should receive a point in the event that both fencers landed touches at about the same time in a phrase.

Riposte—The offensive action by a fencer who successfully parries an attack.

Round Robin—A pool format in which every person fences everyone else once.

Saber—One of the three weapons; touches are ususually made by cutting actions. The valid target area is above the hips including the head and arms but not the hands.

Salle d'Armes—French for a fencing school or club; shortens to "salle."

Second Intention—A tactic in which the attacker makes an action that is intended to be parried so that the attacker can act upon the anticipated riposte by the defender.

Seed—A fencer's rank relative to other fencers in a pool or direct elimination table.

Stop Hit—A thrust (or cut in saber) that is made into an opponent's preparation.

Supination—A fencing hand position or parry in which the palm faces up.

Thrust—A hit from close range made by simply extending the weapon arm.

Touché—(French) An acknowledgment of a touch by the recipient.

Trompement—(French) An attacking action, generally a disengagement or cutover, that deceives an opponent's parry attempt.

U.S.F.A.—The initials of the United States Fencing Association.

U.S.F.C.A.—The initials of the United States Fencing Coaches Association.

White Light—In foil fencing, a light on the scoring apparatus indicating an off target touch.

Yellow Penalty Card—A warning by the referee for the first violation of the rules in a bout.

Yielding Parry—Also called a ceding parry. Instead of resisting a bind attempt, the defender allows the attacker's force to carry the blade to a parry position.

Index